Nightmarish Neighborhood #2

Old Orchard Street & The Petrifying Past of North White Plains

by Eric Pleska

Write On Dudes
Productions

CONTENTS

DON'T BE SCARED,
BE PREPARED

Proceed with caution This collection of true stories about people, places, and events that unfolded on and around Old Orchard Street in North White Plains, NY, holds secrets that may unsettle and shock. This nonfiction book, while rich in local offbeat history, also unveils tales of tragedy, disturbing deaths, eerie events, and perhaps even a lurking monster.

Old Orchard Street is a primarily residential stretch of peaceful scenic suburban road that begins just beyond George Washington Elementary School in the Manhattan suburb of White Plains in Westchester County.

The approximately 2.5-mile-long street runs along the White Plains Reservoir, past the Rocky Ledge Swimming Club, through North White Plains, up to Cranberry Lake, and ends at the intersection with Mt. Kisco Road, with views of the reservoir that now blankets the lost village of Kensico.

This journey takes us through a neighborhood with a dark past, beginning with the Revolutionary War era when General George Washington stayed in town and ending in the present. We will encounter some fascinating local historical figures along the way, including a mysterious hermit, a pioneer of professional wrestling, a bootlegging boss, and even a notorious outlaw.

There are tales of true crime, unsolved mysteries, and possibly an unfound hidden treasure. Our eerie expedition will unfold geographically and cover multiple locations on Old Orchard Street and various past and present sites around North White Plains.

 If you're easily frightened, you may want to stop now. Otherwise, be prepared to discover some of the horrific history on and around a relatively pleasant, scenic suburban street.

1.) KENSICO RESERVOIR

The construction of the immense Kensico Dam caused the village of Kensico, NY, to be evacuated, destroyed, and submerged by the waters of the newly formed Kensico Reservoir in 1917. As a result, only a handful of buildings in Kensico managed to withstand the massive transformation, which essentially turned the quiet farming community into a gigantic lake with a small peninsula and an island composed of demolished homes and wagon trails.

Situated the high ground of Old Orchard Street, the Raven family's Lakeview Hotel in Kensico, NY, was one of the few survivors of the village's evacuation and subsequent destruction. A movie director eventually burned down the once-popular hotel for a film. Before leaving town, John Raven donated the 35-acre property to the Jennie Clarkson Home.

Located at 2 Old Orchard Street in what is now labeled Valhalla, NY, the Jennie Clarkson Home has been an orphanage, group home, and, more recently, a highly-rated facility that provides excellent education and exceptional, coordinated residential treatment services for young people with developmental disabilities. Their secluded campus includes Jennie's Farm, which allows residents to interact and care for a herd of on-site goats, chickens, and donkeys, while enjoying views of the nearby Kensico Reservoir.

After the evacuation of Kensico village and the subsequent completion of Kensico Dam in 1917, the Kensico Dam Plaza became a popular recreation area. Built on a former swamp, the large public park lets visitors enjoy jogging, bicycle riding, and sunbathing. The plaza hosts various events throughout the year, including concerts, cultural festivals, and its annual Winter Wonderland. Visitors can also enjoy views of the reservoir, which Westchester and New York City residents utilize as a source of drinking water.

While it's mostly a peaceful environment, Kensico Dam has experienced some accidental, unfortunate, tragic, and even brutal events throughout time, including the following thirteen terrifying tales.

I

In late August 1925, a reckless driver forced another car off the road above the Kenisco Dam. The sedan plunged down a twenty-foot embankment, crashing through heavy fir trees and into Kensico Lake, where it finally halted and began to sink.

Motorists passed the accident and didn't stop until one car finally did. Driven by White Plain High School champion sprinter George De Nault, his passenger, Richard Craig, sprang into action.

The 17-year-old WPHS student dove into the water and succeeded in opening one of the sedan's doors and pulling the drowning children to safety. After getting the children to safety along the shoreline with George, Richard dove back in to rescue everyone else. He saved all six victims. The WPHS students then drove the six victims to White Plains Hospital before the police or an ambulance could arrive.

The police issued a warrant for Benjamin Bates, the New York City driver of the vehicle that allegedly caused the near-fatal accident. The two White Plains boys vanished from the spotlight, not wanting to be recognized for their heroic efforts. Unfortunately, not all subsequent events had such happy endings.

II

The reservoir is off-limits for swimming; however, on September 3, 1933, five friends from New Rochelle in their 20s decided to ignore the rules. Amongst them was a former petty officer in the merchant marines, 23-year-old Hugh Samuel Jarvis Jr.

Hugh plunged into the water, swam about 15 feet, and sank without calling for help. His friends dove in after but were unable to locate him.

Two of his friends got in their car and headed to the police station for help. On their way back to the reservoir, the automobile skidded, struck a fence and overturned. They escaped unharmed. A few hours later, the police recovered Hugh's body.

III

In January 1934, a 100-pound deer suffering from total blindness fell into the frozen reservoir after the ice cracked beneath her hooves. Witnesses immediately called Armonk police for help, who, after several false starts, managed to rescue the drowning doe.

IV

In late March 1942, a small car crashed through a guard rail on Route 22 near the King Street intersection, plunged down a 10-foot embankment, and landed on its side in Kensico Reservoir. The tragic accident claimed the lives of 18-year-old Frederick Robert Snyder and 24-year-old Frederick Martin Burns Jr., both from White Plains.

V

Shortly past 5:30 am on December 11, 1940, James Restel guided his trailer truck with Massachusetts plates along Route 22, bordering the reservoir. As he neared the intersection with Route 120, he saw a frantic woman alongside the road, her arms outstretched. As he heard her screams for help, the New England trucker jammed on the brakes.

The distressed damsel in her early 30s was dripping wet and shivering without a coat. She was missing a shoe, and her gray wool dress had rips. Her legs were bruised and bloody from her knees to her feet. As she climbed into the truck's cab, she began an incoherent story about what happened as a North Castle police officer approached the scene.

Officer Chester Pietschker wrapped the woman in a blanket and drove her to the nearest doctor. After treatment, she identified as Mrs. Eleanor Strubing of Greenwich, CT. The wife of an advertising executive said:

"Oh, I am happy to be alive! I have been through a frightful night. My houseman must have gone berserk. He was been tormenting me all night with a knife and had raped me. Doctor, do you think I will get pregnant? Do you think I will contract syphilis?"

As the doctor treated her wounds, she told the police that she had been forced to submit to rape by her chauffeur-butler, a 31-year-old Black man from White Plains named Joseph Spell. She said that between 10 pm and 5 am, Spell raped her four times. He then forced her at knife-point to write a "ransom note" demanding $5,000 from her husband. Next, she said Spell bound her wrists and ankles with a cord and carried her through a covered passageway to the garage. He then forcibly threw her into the car and gagged her with a ripped piece of her dress.

He drove to the Bear Gutter Bridge alongside the reservoir. He pulled over and dumped her over a rail into the frigid water. From above, Spell threw stones at the victim as she broke free from her restraints and began to swim. As her fur coat became waterlogged, Spell fled the scene. A short while later, he returned with a flashlight, but by this time, Mrs. Strubing had gone downstream, climbed out of the water, and hid behind some bushes. The attacker left for the second time, and the victim went on the road to seek help.

The police arrested Spell. They found him hiding behind a furnace as his wife slept through the night's events. Spell initially confessed to the attack but denied other charges. Due to the brutal nature of the crime and the forcible "ransom note," a conviction could result in the death penalty.

At trial, Samuel Friedman, an attorney from The National Association for the Advancement of Colored People, represented the accused. In dramatic contrast to Mrs. Strubing's accusations, Mr. Spell not only denied the rape charges but told the all-White jury that Mrs. Strubing seduced him. He also denied binding her or tying her up in any way. In his version of the story, the pair went for a drive, and when they reached Bear Gutter Bridge, he experienced car trouble and pulled over. That's when he says she bolted from the car and ran into the reservoir. Concerned for her safety, he returned to the scene with a flashlight to try to find her. Spell said that when the police initially questioned him, he lied to them because he wasn't sure if they were trying to charge him with rape or murder.

After deliberating for 12 hours and 38 minutes, the jury, comprised of six men and six women, returned a verdict. The court acquitted Mr. Spell on all charges. The ruling surprised many, including the Harrison Police Chief, who had reported that a few months prior, the Harrison police arrested Spell on a charge of trying to extort money from his former employer, Mrs. Loretta Morningstar, in a similar staged ransom manner.

A year later, Spell and his wife relocated to Easton, PA, where they found employment as chauffeur and maid, respectively, in a 30-room mansion belonging to E.J. Fox, a former district attorney. A few months later, the police arrested the couple for grand theft after they stole cash and jewelry.

VI

A Westchester teenager, Edward Haight, became one of the most reviled murderers to ever sit on Sing Sing's death row. In the autumn of 1942, the 16-year-old abducted two young sisters, Margaret and Helen, in a stolen Ford station wagon on the outskirts of Bedford, NY.

A few days later, Connecticut State troopers stopped Edward near Stamford for a traffic violation. The Haight family was well known to the police, with many run-ins with the law. In the 1930s, the police arrested Edward's father and two uncles for numerous Westchester jewelry burglaries. The troopers searched Edward's small, beat-up truck and found a gas ration book from the stolen Ford station wagon.

While in custody, he confessed to the girls' brutal murders. He stated he shoved a handkerchief down the throat of 7-year-old Margaret before mutilating her with a large hunting knife. He kept her body in the car while her 9-year-old sister Helen remained tied up in the backseat. He sexually assaulted Helen in a wooded area, placed the terrified girl under the car, and drove over her several times. The police fished Helen's lifeless body out of Kensico Reservoir and located Margaret's body in a nearby wooded area.

The crimes made national news, which dubbed Edward "The Ravisher." Charged with two counts of 1st-degree murder, Edward not only didn't show remorse but burst into laughter when recounting the crimes in court. On July 8, 1943, he died for his crimes in Sing Sing's electric chair.

VII

A sensational story appeared in the pages of *The Reporter Dispatch* newspaper in the fall of 1956. The "Adventure Editor" who penned the piece stated that two fisherman phoned him to report something mysterious in a cove of Kensico Reservoir. The strange call was followed up by a letter from a Port Chester sportsman who described in great detail the experience of his fishermen friends.

The letter said the men noticed a "log" in the water but thought nothing of it. There was no wind, and the lake's surface was like glass. After a few minutes, they had become aware that the "log" had "drifted" almost across the cove. The two men quickly reeled in and hastened along the edge of the cover to where the object seemed to be heading. They got within 24 feet of it, and both simultaneously realized it wasn't a log. It was an alligator!

It's unclear how the four-foot-long alligator got into the reservoir or what became of it. Strangely, years later, during the summer of 1982, fishermen spotted a two-foot-long alligator in the reservoir. This time, the Department of Environmental Conversation was able to catch the animal. Named "Kensy," the reptile was donated to the nearby Bronx Zoo.

Water Supply patrolman Anthony Ploutz confirmed in 1983 that there had been no alligator sightings since. A year after Kensy's capture, they got occasional "crazy stories from guys fishing at night. They're out there in the darkness, and raccoons turn into mountain lions."

VIII

In March 1981, the police recovered the body of a 46-year-old man from Yonkers on the North Castle side of the reservoir. The police said the man was wearing a suit, tie, and raincoat when found. They located his car in the same area, on the western side of the dam. It remains unclear if the death was accidental or suicide. However, the medical examiner ruled out foul play.

IX

On May 31, 1983, a 20-year-old Thornwood man died after he jumped from the top of the dam. Witnesses told Mount Pleasant Police that the victim walked onto the dam's causeway, perched on the concrete wall, and then jumped off, falling more than 300 feet onto the grassy plaza below.

X

A few days later, on June 2, 1983, a 65-year-old White Plains woman drowned in the reservoir. A North White Plains fisherman spotted her body floating near the shore, dressed in gray slacks and a gold shirt. The North Castle Police didn't find any identification on her person but were able to figure out her identity after contacting White Plains Police about recent missing persons reports. Medical examiner Dr. Louis Roh determined there was no foul play involved, and the drowning was not accidental.

XI

Just a few days after that tragedy, a 28-year-old man from Thornwood fatally plunged off the Kensico Dam. The police said he was friends with the Thornwood man who had jumped from the dam a few weeks prior.

XII

In August 1984, North Castle police scuba divers recovered the body of a 56-year-old Yonkers fisherman. The victim slipped from a rock into the Kensico Reservoir at the base of the Route 22 bridge. Police said there was evidence the man had been drinking before the accident.

XIII

In July 1990, the North Castle Police had a tragic mystery to solve. They received a report that a fisherman from White Plains spotted a partly decomposed body in a sleeping bag about 40 feet from shore near Route 120 and Route 22. The medical examiner said the tattooed corpse had been in the water for at least two weeks. Because the body of the unknown man was found with his hands and feet tied, the police began investigating the situation as a homicide.

A month later, after successfully solving numerous clues, North Castle Police Chief Fred Gambino was able to identify the victim as James Scott, a 23-year-old rifleman of the British Army.

With the help of Scotland Yard, the local police tracked Scott and a fellow British soldier named Adrian Mann from their base in Osnabruck, West Germany, to Woodbridge, VA. It's unclear why the pair went AWOL; however, a car the duo purchased turned up abandoned in Chicago.

The police viewed the strange crime as a gigantic, tough-to-solve puzzle. Chief Gambino pointed to Mann as a likely suspect based on his being the last known person to see Scott alive. Chief Gambino later revealed that Scott was found in a military-style sleeping bag weighed down by rocks tied to his feet.

"This appears to be two friends who apparently didn't get along too well, and we think that one did the other one in," Gambino said. However, it's unclear what brought the pair to the Kensico Reservoir.

Scotland Yard questioned Mann, who was serving time for desertion charges in a British prison. Scott, who wore tattoos of symbols of his native Scotland, was buried in his homeland.

 Two years later, a North Castle detective received an anonymous phone call. The mysterious caller provided specific information about the homicide, leading the detective to believe the person had first-hand knowledge about the case. He said the phone call was traced to a pay phone at Croton Point Park and publically urged the caller to make contact with him again.

2.) THE CRANBERRY CREATURE

The entrance to the Cranberry Lake Reserve is just a few yards away from the Jennie Clarkson Home. The lake is surrounded by dense woods which used to be called The Cranberry Forest by the locals of Kensico, NY. In the fall of 1894, residents reported the presence of something strange living in the dark forest.

Numerous petrified Kensico, NY residents reported hearing the eerie, ominous sounds of the mysterious creature in September 1894. A few weeks later, the sightings began. Frantic witnesses described seeing a gigantic hairy brown beast that unleashes a booming growl lurking in the darkness of The Cranberry Forest. It's believed the creature lives in the densely wooded area above Kensico Lake (now Kensico Reservoir) near Cranberry Lake. The beast has struck fear in locals as it's said to have even survived gunshot wounds.

While witnesses cannot identify the creature, its presence is responsible for widespread alarm and panic. Many women and children have been too scared to go out at night, reminiscent of when a ferocious panther escaped from a Connecticut circus and unleashed havoc and fear in the neighborhood years prior. Frightened men carried sharp weapons like bush scythes for protection.

John and Caroline Raven's children were frightened by the sounds of the hairy beast near the family's Lake Side Hotel. The creature's growls and shrieks were unmistakable and terrifying. Even the parents were horrified when they heard the sounds.

The Raven family had lived in the area for years and were used to the noises and creatures of the nearby woods. However, they knew that this was not the sound of a fox, owl, coyote, black bear, or wildcat, which have all been loose in the woods before.

John Raven and one of his coworkers armed themselves with rifles and headed toward the dark woods to investigate some eerie sounds. They traced the shrieks and growls to a location about 200 yards away from the hotel.

The Cranberry Forest and the surrounding woods are known to have housed various infamous hermits. Some of them used to sleep in caves near the search area. One of the more renowned hermits, The Leatherman, was known to speak only a few words. When John and his coworker reached the source of the terrifying noises, they were confident that the sounds were not of human origin.

Led by a dog, the armed duo marched eastward into the woods. When they got close to the source of the noises, the dog dashed out of sight into a thicket. A few moments later, the men heard the growls and shrieks, followed by the loud yelping of their dog, who retreated out of the dark brush, refusing to reenter.

The next night, a Kensico hunting party, including Charles Mosher, Robert Mosher, and Bob Hart, ventured after the monster. Armed with weapons, a dog led them to the spot where Mr. Raven had his encounter.

By 11 pm, there was no trace of the beast. To induce the hiding hairy savage, Charles Mosher began roaring at the top of his lungs. Soon after, something echoed the roars from the thickets near Cranberry Lake.

The dog charged into the woods, wildly barking as if circling the enemy. And then, the men saw it. Before them was an open space, and as they watched, something broke cover on the left and moved into the open.

The men reported seeing a creature that resembled a gorilla. It was walking on two legs one moment and on all fours the next. They described it as oversized, brown, and hairy but couldn't get a good view of its neck and head. They were uncertain about what it was but aimed their guns towards it. After the smoke cleared, the creature was nowhere to be seen.

The following day, they returned to the spot and found peculiar footprints in the sand where the beast had crossed the old wood road. Mosher said the prints looked like a human hand, with indistinct fingers and a widely separated thumb mark.

What happened a night or two later was even more startling. Charles Mosher and Mr. Hart were hunting raccoons in the woods. While creeping on their prey, they almost tripped over the monstrous creature they searched for the night before. Their dog launched at the silent creature, who was perhaps taking a nap. The dog sprang at its throat. Instead of biting the dog or retreating, the beast caught it in a crooked forearm and hurled it against a tree. The men, too shaken to consider engaging in combat, dashed out of the woods to safety.

The Cranberry Creature remained at large, terrorizing the residents of Kensico. Perhaps even spookier is that if scared citizens manage to escape its vicious grip and return to the safety of their homes, locals claim to have spotted the mysterious monster peeking into their windows!

In late October 1929, over 200 acres of woodlands extending from Kensico Reservoir to Cranberry Lake was completely burned. Firefighters battled the raging blaze for eight hours and later determined the cause was a lit cigarette tossed on a pile of leaves.

Some believe the Cranberry Creature may have been some prophetic being similar to The Mothman of West Virginia, sent from beyond to warn of impending doom.

3.)CRANBERRY LAKE

Former North Castle Town Clerk Joseph Miller wrote that before building Kensico Dam, the area that became North White Plains had a population of only sixteen families. As a result of the Dam construction, North White Plains' population exploded. New residents were transplanted from the flooded Village of Kensico, and workers who came to build the dam became new residents. One of the area's most popular attractions is the Cranberry Lake Preserve.

Cranberry Lake Preserve is a nearly 200-acre park operated by the Westchester County Department of Parks & Recreation. Although it neighbors the Jennie Clarkson Home at 1700 Old Orchard Street in Valhalla, NY, the Preserve's address is 1609 Old Orchard Street in West Harrison, NY.

Since the 1960s, the park has been a haven for animals and plants, including migratory birds, turtles, and dragonflies. There are also populations of vultures, snakes, and a rare breed of bark-eating beetles, first discovered in 1921 by Dr. M.W. Blackman at The Preserve.

Within the grounds are a variety of habitats, including a four-acre lake, mixed hardwood forest, vernal pools, and a swamp. There are also several ponds, a mysterious stone chamber, an old quarry, and various abandoned things, like an old tennis court and a collection of junked automobiles. The site has also been the setting of multiple tragic events.

The stone quarry area once contained a sandpit, a stone-crushing plant, and 17 miles of railroad tracks leading to Kensico Dam. The Kensico Dam has as much masonry as some of Egypt's iconic pyramids, which workers sourced from the quarry on Old Orchard Street between 1911 and 1917.

The first blast in the quarry occurred in 1913. A dozen huge derricks were used to lift and load large stones for the face of the Kensico Dam. During two months in 1914, 32.5 tons of dynamite were loaded into the rock, creating the quarry's most enormous blast, breaking up approximately 117,000 cubic yards of rocks, weighing over 179 million pounds. The job included using horses, mules, steam shovels, and steam engines called "Dinkys." The small gauge railroad transported sand, gravel, and granite the workers used to build the dam. An old wheel and axel are displayed along The Preserve's purple nature trail on a piece of the original railroad.

The quarry has led to the formation of a unique habitat from years of rainwater, which has created small ponds over time. In June 1922, local police found an abandoned car in a flooded quarry pond. They determined that the car had been stolen from someone in Yonkers but could not determine whether the vehicle's driver or passenger(s) had gone down with it. The police were first notified about the car after being discovered by two young boys playing near the site.

According to local legend, after the completion of Kensico Dam, a popular way to dispose of old, unwanted automobiles was to send them over the quarry cliffs. A few years after the Dam was built, the police implicated three juveniles, including two 15-year-olds from West Harrison, in creating an "automobile graveyard" in a wooded area off Buckout Road. The cars, some of which had been stolen, were driven at high speeds during impromptu demolition derbies. Afterward, the participants junked the wrecked vehicles in the woods. White Plains Detectives discovered the "graveyard" of about 20 demolished cars after three were set on fire, creating smoke and flames in the area.

On September 26, 1927, a group of seven young Boy Scouts from Mt. Vernon went on a hike in The Preserve without adult consent or supervision. During their adventure, the boys decided to swim in one of the abandoned quarry ponds. While in the cold water, a thirteen-year-old boy named Frank Govin Jr began experiencing leg cramps. Unable to move, he drowned.

Two years later, an eerily similar tragedy occurred in the same location. In August 1929, two White Plains boys, Morris Isaacs and James Donnelly, went swimming at the quarry around 3 pm. While near the shore, Isaacs suddenly seized with a cramp and sank. Donnelly grabbed his pal by the heel but could not draw him to the surface. Troopers dragged through the deep lake with grappling hooks in an attempt to recover the boy's body. They were unsuccessful. They then tried using dynamite to dislodge the body from the bottom of the quarry. They were unsuccessful.

In July 1937, the police recovered the body of drowning victim Joseph Sgoia in Cranberry Lake. The 18-year-old from The Bronx was the son of a popular butcher on White Plains Road.

In 1942, local police reported that a White Plains tree surgeon and his 17-year-old nephew drowned in Cranberry Lake after their frail homemade rowboat capsized. Neither of the victims, 41-year-old Walter Wells from Lake Street or Herbert Delaney from Old Orchard Street, could swim. Local police and firefighters used grappling hooks in the 20-foot-deep water for nearly two hours to recover the victims' bodies.

In 1954, Old Orchard Street resident Lillian Rose Sochurek, the neighbor of professional wrestling superstar Arnold "Golden Boy" Skaaland, purchased 29 acres of the quarry lands, including its ponds. The largest of the quarry ponds became reinvented as a swimming pool, the main attraction of the newly branded Birchwood Swim Club. Operational through the 1990s, the popular neighborhood summer-time attraction also included tennis courts.

During the 1990s, Westchester County bought 23 acres of land to add to the Cranberry Lake Preserve, including the parcel owned by Lillian. When the county purchased the grounds, it allowed the swim club to continue operating for five years. After that, the fine print of the property deed would cause a problem; unless its neighbors agreed to it, usage as a public swimming pool would be prohibited.

In 1997, after several neighbors, including a multi-millionaire socialite, objected to the continuing operation of the Birchwood Swimming Club, the Westchester Board of Legislators shut down the park after declaring it "a passive park."

Despite numerous tragedies and the swimming pool's closure, The Cranberry Lake Preserve remains a popular attraction. Several productions have filmed scenes at the picture-esque preserve, including the NBC drama *Manifest* and the Netflix series *Maniac*, which shot scenes there in 2017 with Academy Award winners Sally Field and Emma Stone.

4.) RYE LAKE

Neighboring the Cranberry Lake Preserve main entrance at 1606 Old Orchard Street in West Harrison is the Southern Westchester BOCES Rye Lake Campus. BOCES, an acronym for Boards of Cooperative Education Services, is a public organization created by the New York State Legislature in 1948 to provide shared educational programs and services to school districts. Bordering the campus is a body of water that connects to Kensico Reservoir named Rye Lake.

Unfortunately, Rye Lake has also been the site of multiple fatal tragedies dating back to an accident in August 1870 during a summer picnic in a grove adjacent to the lake. In the middle of the afternoon, a 14-year-old boy named Jacob Roach and two young girls, who were sisters, went swimming. One of the Hart sisters slipped on a smooth rock and fell into the lake, which was thirty feet deep. Jacob dove in and attempted to rescue the drowning girl. He succeeded in twice bringing her to the surface, but finding nothing to cling to and becoming exhausted, the two finally sank together and drowned. The bodies were recovered shortly afterward and buried together in the same grave.

Sadly, just a few years later, in July 1877, 19-year-old Charles Fardon also drowned in Rye Lake. He had been celebrating the 4th of July, fishing with another boy on the lake that afternoon. Being unable to swim, Charles ventured out too far, stepped off a treacherous ledge, and sank into deep water. A local man tried to rescue the well-liked

Alexander Institute student but couldn't reach him in time.

In October 1880, a local man took his horse to the lake for a drink. Unfortunately, the horse stepped too far off a bank on the lake's shore, which had a sudden drop. The horse, the wagon it was pulling, and the man sank about 30 feet to the bottom. Miraculously, the man soon arose to the surface and was helped ashore by nearby witnesses who rushed to help.

Witnesses all assumed the horse drowned because his owner harnessed him to a wagon. Moments later, against all odds, the brave horse broke free from the harness and made it safely to shore. After considerable labor, a team of locals fished the wagon out of the lake with ropes and chains.

Later in 1880, several farmers reported a loose wild cat in the Rye Lake vicinity. At first, locals were unclear if it was a bobcat, mountain lion, or something else responsible for the killings of multiple calves. As time progressed, as discussed in *Nightmarish Neighborhood #1*, it turned out to be an escaped panther from a traveling circus. The panther made its way from Connecticut to Westchester, terrorizing the residents of Kensico and the nearby neighborhoods.

A few years after the escaped panther wreaked havoc on the neighborhood for several months, people around Rye Lake reported seeing two loose wildcats. They had been pets of Herman Clarke, who lived in Port Chester. He kept the wild animals in a cage, which they managed to escape. Attempting not to alarm the residents of Port Chester, Mr. Clarke and his sons kept the news quiet. Unfortunately, that decision led to problems at Rye Lake.

 A few days later, a local farmer, Samuel Adams, went hunting near Rye Lake with his dogs. He heard a large hiss above him, and a wildcat sprang from the limb of a tree. Adams jumped aside in time to avoid being killed. The dogs tackled the wildcat; although there were three dogs, they were no match for the vicious feline. Adams could not get a clear rifle shot at the cat without risking his dogs' lives. Suddenly, the cat jumped at him and sank its sharp teeth and claws into his neck. He tore it away from him, threw it on the ground, and shot it dead. Locals organized a hunt for the second cat, but it managed to evade capture.

 During the 1890s, local fishermen noticed that hordes of dead fish were floating on Rye Lake's surface. A deeper investigation revealed that unknown persons were throwing dynamite into the water.

 In a tragic tale, in 1899, a local Russian man named Julius Waskiesenki allegedly contemplated suicide. He removed his shoes, placed them under a tree, and dove into Rye Lake with the intent of drowning himself. Luckily, Julius regretted his melancholy decision and, escaped the lake's waters and returned to shore.

Unfortunately, he lay there for several days without any food. Two local men found his body, reduced to skin and bones, face downward in some underbrush. Before his death, Julius scribbled on a piece of paper: *"I landed in New York two weeks ago from Russia and have been looking for work ever since. Spent all my money and was without food for a week. Let me die."*

Sadly, in July 1914, a businessman from upstate New York jumped from the 90-foot concrete bridge over Rye Lake near the Kensico Dam construction site. He fatally plunged into 30 feet of water. It took rescuers six hours to recover his body.

On November 5, 1937, a 29-year-old steelworker named James Lodge from Poughkeepsie, NY, fell off a concrete ledge beneath the Rye Bridge, plummeting 75 feet into the frigid waters below, where he drowned. When the police recovered his body from Rye Lake, an officer said he was the third person to die in the reservoir's waters within the month.

In August 1993, just weeks after the discovery of James Scott's body in the Kensico Reservoir, the local police had another tragic mystery to try and solve. While conducting a routine drill in Rye Lake, a police diving team inadvertently discovered the partially decomposed body of a woman.

The police could not determine the woman's age, race, or hair color and reported there was no obvious cause of death. Strangely, nearby, the diving team found a 22-caliber rifle on the south side of the Route 22 bridge.

Within a few weeks, detectives were able to identify the victim as a Suffolk County (Long Island) architect named Marcie Liebler, who had gone missing over five years ago. North Castle police reported that Marcie's husband, 32-year-old Robert Liebler, murdered his wife after a domestic dispute and then dumped her body into Rye Lake. Shortly after, Robert shot himself.

The discovery of Marcie's body was the second time a murder victim's body was recovered from the waters of Rye Lake. As discussed in *Nightmarish Neighborhood #1*, following the disappearance of Kensico farmer Henry Woodman, his body was recovered in a cove on the edge of Rye Lake in 1893. The cove on the outskirts of what is now Park Lane in West Harrison was renamed Woodman's Cove in his honor. His murder remains unsolved.

The thick woods bordering Rye Lake are also home to a legendary hidden treasure guarded by the ghost of a female Revolutionary War-era hermit.

According to legend, written about in local newspapers in 1868 and 1874, an elderly woman from Ireland named "Aunt" Betty Thompson lived in a moss-covered stone hut near Rye Lake during the American Revolution. During the war, Betty was a favorite with the soldiers, who often did their laundry on a shelving rock along the west shore of Rye Lake, which became known as "Betty's Rocks."

Betty lived beyond her 100th birthday. However, following her eventual passing, her home rapidly fell into disrepair. Rocks fell on top of the hut, and it eventually collapsed. The area's oldest residents recalled Betty had large sums of money during her lifetime, but none knew what she did with it. Some people believe that her treasure of silver and gold coins remains buried under her hut's rubble.

At the time, nobody dared recover the treasure mainly because the large rocks were too heavy to move, but also because of the spooky urban legend that every effort to recover the buried loot causes old Betty's ghost to rise from her grave and haunt the treasure hunters. The location of the Rye Lake stone hut has since been lost to time, perhaps one day to be rediscovered.

5.)PLANE CRASHES

The waters of Rye Lake follow the northern edge of Old Orchard Street from the Southern Westchester BOCES campus down the street and through to Park Lane. The water surrounds a mass of land now known as Great Island. The island is the largest in Westchester County but used to be something quite different: a steep hill in the lost Village of Kensico.

Before 1917, locals referred to what is now a 723-acre island as Archer's Hill. Numerous Kensico, NY farms, homes, and stores were located on and around Archer's Hill, which the man-made Rye Lake now surrounds. The island is now strictly off-limits and is home to a large population of venomous copperhead snakes. It's also rumored to be the resting place of Native American leaders who cursed the land after the White man violated an agreement about not destroying particular trees. Perhaps even scarier than deadly snakes and Siwanoy hexes is that Great Island and the surrounding area have been the site of multiple plane crashes, some fatal.

Just behind the island was the county's first airport, Armonk Airport. With humble beginnings on an apple orchard in 1925, the small airport became home to early aviation vehicles like biplanes and barnstormers. In 1927, the airport experienced its first crash in an orchard near The Log Cabin restaurant in North White Plains.

That same year, Charles Lindbergh gained national attention after becoming the first man to fly solo across the Atlantic Ocean in his iconic airplane, "The Spirit of St. Louis". A year later, he appeared at the Armonk Airport to meet fans.

The airport became home to popular air shows that attracted thousands of spectators. Professional stunt flying and parachuting were among the most popular attractions at the airport, including daredevil stunts such as standing on the wings of planes and flying under the Rye Lake Bridge. The iconic Goodyear Blimp also made an appearance as did arguably the most famous aviator of all time, Amelia Earhart.

In 1931, Miss Earhart married publisher George Putnam, and the couple resided on Locust Avenue on the border of Harrison and Rye, NY. Earhart set numerous records in aviation, authored best-selling books about her flying experiences, endorsed products (including her luggage brand), and played a crucial role in establishing The Ninety-Nines, an organization for female pilots. At the peak of her fame, she was arguably the most famous person in the world.

Shortly after becoming the first woman to fly solo across the Atlantic in 1932, local dignitaries held a ceremony to unveil a monument in her honor. The piece, which includes a bronze plaque with a propeller attached to a stone, still stands in a small Harrison park near the train station and is the only one she ever saw during her lifetime.

In 1934, a fire destroyed Amelia's home on Locust Avenue. The blaze destroyed family treasures and personal mementos. The street was later renamed Amelia Earhart Lane in her honor.

Amelia announced in 1937, at age 39, that she would be retiring from the skies after completing one final flight. Her goal was to become the first woman to fly around the world. On July 2, 1937, Amelia and her navigator, Fred Noonan, took off from New Guinea toward Howland Island, one of the last stops on her attempt to circumnavigate the globe. Amelia, Fred, and their Lockheed Electra disappeared shortly after takeoff, and Miss Earhart vanished into legend. Search and rescue missions have come up empty, and the subject remains a popular source of conspiracy theories.

Westchester was also home to another famous female aviation pioneer. In 1939, one year after Amelia Earhart's disappearance, her friend and fellow record-breaking female pilot, Ruth Nichols, helped coordinate a memorial service at Playland Pier. She flew over the crowd to scatter rose petals in her friend's honor. Nichols, who grew up in Rye and attended school in Dobbs Ferry, was also a founding member of The 99's.

In 1928, at age 27, Ruth completed the first nonstop flight from New York to Miami. She broke Charles Lindbergh's transcontinental record in 1930, shaving an hour off his time. By 1931, Ruth had three major international women's records for speed, distance, and altitude. While her accomplishments were impressive, when interviewers talked to Nichols after her flights, they noted that she spoke less about herself and more about the potential of the field of aeronautics to revolutionize our world. She was analytical, articulate, and dedicated, earning her a leadership position in general aviation promotion for the Fairchild Aviation Corporation.

As her record-setting successes continued, Ruth dreamed of becoming the first woman to cross the Atlantic in flight. With her sight on the goal, tragedy hit. In July 1931, she crashed soon after takeoff in Canada while attempting her first transatlantic flight. She was severely injured but optimistic, promising to fly again as soon as she recovered. When she returned home, flown on a stretcher and still in a plaster cast, She told reporters, "They can't keep me down." She crashed again in October 1931, parachuting out of a burning plane in Louisville, Kentucky. Despite setbacks, Nichols was courageous and determined. A year later, when Amelia broke the record, Ruth supported her. Unfortunately, by 1960, she suffered from depression and, at age 59, died in New York City after an overdose of barbiturates.

Despite the popularity of its local air shows, the Armonk Airport eventually ceased operations. A new and larger airport took its place nearby. Opened in 1942 during World War II, Westchester County Airport was initially home to an Air National Guard unit to protect New York City and the Kensico Reservoir. Located just 4 miles from Old Orchard Street, the airport's towers of electric markers are just behind Great Island.

In 1948, the 137th Fighter Squadron of the New York Air National Guard received Federal recognition and officially began military operations at the new airport. The unit was initially equipped with the F-47 Thunderbolt aircraft and provided many years of loyal service to the United States, flying missions both stateside and overseas. The unit also had an F-51 Mustang and a versatile all-weather interceptor known as The F-9 Starfire.

Westchester County Airport's first scheduled airline flights were by American Airlines in late 1949, and the first scheduled jet flight was a Mohawk BAC One-Eleven in 1965. The airport would grow to become the 4th busiest airport in New York State, but sadly, multiple tragedies occurred in the neighborhood, including the following sixteen incidents.

I

In 1950, 26-year-old National Guard pilot Lt. Robert Pellicane was killed after his F47 Thunderbolt careened out of control and crashed to the ground while trying to land at Westchester County Airport. The fatal plane crash was the first since the airport opened in 1943. The scene of the accident, a field near Rye Lake, was closely guarded because the plane reportedly had secret equipment aboard.

II

In a hillside crash on December 12, 1967, near White Plains, a two-engine airplane went out of control because of fuel starvation. While en route to Westchester County Airport from Williamsport, PA, the plane fell from the sky near the White Plains police firing range on Old Orchard Street during a heavy fog. The pilot, 62-year-old Alexander Somers, the vice president of Central International Elevator Co. in New York City, died in the crash.

III

 A plane crash on November 20, 1974, claimed the lives of four victims. The single-engine Cessna 182 was on a flight from Teterboro, NJ, to White Plains and crashed into a heavily wooded area about two miles north of the Westchester County Airport runway. Federal Aviation Administration officials said they lost radar contact with the plane at 8 pm. An hour later, area police officers found the wreckage near Route 22 and Cooney Hill Road on the edge of Rye Lake.

IV

On January 16, 1976, a small Cessna plane crashed in a wooded area near the Kensico Reservoir, killing the 20-year-old pilot from Rockford, Illinois, and injuring three passengers

V

 In February 1981, a plane crashed on Great Island. Six passengers and two pilots perished in the crash. Searchers found the wreckage scattered in mud, snow, and thick underbrush in the woods near the Dark Hollow side of the island. A spokesman for the Federal Aviation Administration, Robert Fulton, said in a *New York Times* article from February 2, 1981, "People at the airport reported seeing a fireball in that area." Nancy Witherspoon, whose house faces the site of the crash, said: "It was a huge, rosy color. It looked like White Plains was on fire."

VI

In 1988, a New Rochelle man and his three children died after their single-engine Beechcraft Bonanza crashed into the woods near Old Orchard Street shortly after takeoff from the Westchester County airport.

VII

A crash just before midnight killed a Massachusetts couple on November 15, 1989, after their single-engine Piper Arrow Cherokee crashed on Great Island as it approached the airport. A teenage passenger from Yorktown survived the horrific ordeal with non-life-threatening injuries.

VIII

In June 1990, a Cessna Twin Engine Skymaster crashed into Rye Lake, and the disaster claimed the lives of a 70-year-old man from Mount Vernon and his grandson.

IX

In April 1994, a pilot swam to safety after losing power and crashing into Rye Lake following an aborted landing attempt at Westchester Airport. Several motorists pulled off the highway after seeing the plane drop from the sky.

A limousine driver watched from the woods as the plane sank. He told reporters, "When I got here, the bubbles were still coming up - it was all white. All of a sudden, I saw him break loose from the plane and start swimming."

The plane completely sank into the lake within five minutes, but the pilot swam steadily as about a half dozen onlookers waited on shore. As he approached shore, rescuers threw him a rope and helped him to safety. Armonk firefighters treated the 48-year-old pilot on the shore of Rye Lake before he was taken to St. Agnes Hospital.

X

A cockpit fire forced the pilot of a single-engine Cessna to make an emergency landing near the Westchester County Airport in May 1996 as the plane approached the airport. A rescue party pulled the injured pilot and solo passenger from Rye Lake.

X I

On June 22, 2001, a Florida man missed his first attempt to land in heavy morning fog at the county airport and crashed his Piper Saratoga into the nearby woods on the outskirts of Buckout Road. Later that year, a Beech Sierra crashed just north of the airport, killing the pilot.

XII

On April 23, 2005, a practice flight ended in tragedy after a Cessna 172 propeller plane slammed into the woods near Rye Lake and burst into flames, killing the flight instructor and student pilot.

XIII

On June 18, 2011, a Manhattan family and teenage friend aboard a small Cessna 210 died after the airplane suddenly crashed while trying to make an emergency landing in the woods near Westchester Airport. The six-seat, single-engine plane reported to the airport control tower that it had to make an emergency landing just a minute after it took off at 1:04 pm. The aircraft turned back around and was making a loop when it crashed, landing in a watershed near the corporate headquarters of Mastercard.

XIV

On November 16, 2013, a single-engine Beechcraft returning to the airport from Pittsburgh landed hard on its belly in a King Street office complex parking lot in Armonk. Fortunately, the pilot only suffered minor injuries.

XV

In June 2014, David Rockefeller's son Richard died tragically in a plane he was piloting that crashed in a residential neighborhood near Westchester County Airport. The Piper Meridian single-engine turboprop aircraft left the Westchester County Airport at about 8 am. The plane was reported down within 10 minutes in a residential area less than 3 miles away in Purchase, NY. The aircraft came within 20 feet of hitting a house, crashing in front of horse stables on residential property.

Richard, the great-grandson of John D. Rockefeller, who founded Standard Oil, was a skilled pilot who regularly flew out of the Westchester County Airport. It's believed that a heavy fog the morning of takeoff played a role in the tragic accident that claimed the life of the 65-year-old pilot. Richard Rockefeller was president of the Rockefeller Brothers Fund, chairman of the Doctors Without Borders' U.S. Advisory Board for over 20 years, and a board member of Rockefeller University. He practiced medicine in Falmouth and Portland, Maine, and was married with two children and two stepchildren.

XV

Pilot Boruch Taub and his passenger Benjamin Chafetz died when the single-engine Beechcraft A36 crashed about 1.5 miles from the Westchester County Airport on January 19, 2023. The Cleveland residents were heading from JFK Airport to the Cuyahoga County Airport in Richmond Heights, OH. The pilot reported engine trouble, including a lack of vertical speed, while unsuccessfully trying to climb to 8,000 feet in elevation. Moments later, the pilot, in communication with ground control, declared, "Mayday! Mayday! Mayday!"

As per *The New York Post*,

"Understand. The airport is just behind you now. You want to start a left turn if you can. I'm seeing a right turn," the controller says. You're set up perfectly for a left base to Runway 16, 11 o'clock, just under 2 miles. You look beautiful for the left base for Runway 16," he adds.

However, the pilot appears to be having increasing difficulty.
"If you can keep giving me vectors. I can't see a thing out here,"

In one of the final transmissions, the controller says: "You wanna correct back to the left for the runway at your 10 o'clock." He adds, tragically, "Radar contact lost."

The Jewish Chronicle reported:
Shortly before the crash, Chafetz managed to send a text message to a WhatsApp temple prayer group, apparently believing he was giving a private farewell to his wife.

"I love you and the kids. I am sorry for everything I have done. We lost engines. Call and have the community say Tehillim,"

Searchers found wreckage from the fatal disaster in a heavily wooded area on Cooley Hill Road, near the northern tip of Rye Lake by Great Island.

6.)WILLIAM MULDOON

During the late 1800s, one of the neighborhood's most famous residents was professional wrestling pioneer and health club creator William Muldoon. Known as "The Solid Man", Muldoon was a Civil War veteran, a former New York City police officer, the founder of the Police Athletic League, and after defeating French wrestling star Andre Christol in 1877, the first Wolrd Wrestling Greco Roman Champion.

Born to Irish immigrants in 1845, Muldoon was already a Civil War veteran by age 20. A year after the War ended, in 1865, he worked as a bouncer in New York City. There, he encountered a man with a black eye and inquired what had happened, which led him to Harry Hill's Saloon and Variety Theater on 26 East Houston Street in Manhattan.

In 1854, promoter Harry Hill converted a two-story grocery store into a saloon, concert, and entertainment hall. The venue combined many entertainment pastimes into a single experience, all while selling alcohol. At one end of the saloon was a stage featuring musicians, puppet shows, and short plays.

Hill was a boxer and a boxing promoter, so naturally, he ran live fights at his venue, which patrons gambled on. Blacks, dancing girls, prostitutes, and well-dressed visitors all took it in. The venue became so popular that many famous names like P.T. Barnum and Mark Twain and frequented it. Thomas Edison even helped install the electrical lighting.

The first-ever gloved boxing champion, John Sullivan, made his fighting debut at Harry Hill's and became a featured attraction. He was the last recognized bare-knuckle champion of his era and had a top drawing fight, beating Steve Taylor at the saloon. Regular fighters at the saloon included Civil War veteran "The Green Mountain Boy" John McMahon, the first female boxing champion, Nell Saunders, famed Collar & Elbow star George W. Flag, and Black fighters like Albert Ellis, "The Professor" Charles Hadley, "Black Sam" Viro Small, and eventually William Muldoon.

As Harry Hill's establishment grew popular, a competing business started nearby. Former boxer Owney Geoghegan opened a tavern called Bastille of the Bowery. The bar contained two rings for boxing and wrestling contests and was notorious for crooked management, rowdy patrons, and an overall seedy atmosphere. Geoghegan reportedly won a decision over an opponent in the Bowery by having his henchmen aim a gun at the referee's head after the fight.

Hill raised the bar of competition by booking predetermined wrestling bouts at his Variety Theater. By having predetermined winners, Hill could produce engaging contests while minimizing injury risk to his stars. John McMahon and William Muldoon were amongst the first to compete in these matches.

By utilizing gimmicky nicknames like "The Solid Man" and wearing a gladiator costume to the ring, William Muldoon may have been the first professional wrestler to add theatrics to his matches. Hill's concept and Muldoon's ideas caught the attention of P.T. Barnum, who later recruited John McMahon and Variety Theater wrestler Ed Decker to tour the country with his traveling circus in similar predetermined bouts. Barnum became the first to create fictitious back stories for wrestlers.

Harry Hill saw the potential of professional wrestling and risked taking it to a larger stage than his converted grocery store: Madison Square Garden. In January 1880, at Manhattan's famous arena, then known as Gilmore Garden, four thousand fans watched as William Muldoon defeated Theo Bauer to become the Greco-Roman Wrestling Champion. Harry Hill served as the referee.

Muldoon and Hill were also early promotion pioneers. During the 1880s, the first newspaper with a sports column was *The Police Gazette*. Conveniently, Harry Hill was friends with its publishers, Richard Fox and Joseph Pulitzer, who gave Muldoon consistent positive press coverage. After Muldoon defeated American Wrestling Champion "Young" Edwin Bibby, Fox wrote, "Muldoon is the first World Champion in modern-day wrestling." To make it official, *The Police Gazette* presented Muldoon with a gold pin symbolizing the honor.

Muldoon continued a successful wrestling career, defeating numerous competitors, including "The Omaha Demon" Clarence Whistler, Colonel J.H. McLaughlin, Carl Sandow, and sumo star Sarakichi Matsuda. He was also involved in the first-ever Boxer vs. Wrestler Match against John Sullivan. After Muldoon body slammed his opponent, the match was declared a No-Contest and 2,000 fans stormed the ring.

New York City Mayor Abram Hewitt shut down Harry Hill's venue in 1886. A year later, Muldoon pivoted to acting. He appeared on stage as The Fighting Gaul in the 1887 Broadway production of Spartacus and in Madame Modjeska's production of Shakespeare's As You Like It alongside the legendary Maurice Barrymore.

Following his 1890 victory over Evan "Strangler" Lewis, Muldoon officially retired from professional wrestling. He symbolically passed his championship to his protégé, Ernest Roeber, who feuded with Lewis.

In 1890, Muldoon purchased the Thomas Carhart mansion in White Plains. He lived at the estate for about a decade before relocating to Purchase, NY, a few years later. Muldoon opened the nation's first fitness center at his new home, around the corner from Old Orchard Street near the intersection of Purchase St and Barnes Lane.

Known by various names, including William Muldoon's Hygienic Institute, The Health Farm, and The Olympia, it became a famed destination for individuals desiring to improve their health. The country's first personal trainer, Muldoon, significantly influenced the health and exercise routines of those who visited his facility. He even offered clients the opportunity to stay at his facility for multiple nights, like a modern-day resort.

Secretary of State Elihu Root, boxing legend John Sullivan, publisher Ralph Pulitzer, and famous actor John Barrymore were among his clients. His workout sessions often featured a mixture of horseback riding with hiking, weight lifting, and tossing around one of Muldoon's inventions, the medicine ball.

The large leather balls weighed between three and six pounds and were tossed back and forth between participants. The throwing techniques varied, engaging all the muscles in the body. The ball-throwing sessions lasted for twenty minutes, after which the participants would rest and drink a pint of hot water. They would then have a plain yet substantial breakfast, keeping health in mind.

Muldoon's popularity grew so great that in 1907, there was talk about him joining President Theodore Roosevelt's cabinet to oversee physical health. In 1921, Governor Nathan Lewis Miller selected Muldoon as the first chairman of The New York State Athletic League, which still oversees professional wrestling and boxing events in New York State.

On June 3, 1933, at his home, William Muldoon died at age 81 from terminal cancer. Former world heavyweight boxing champions Jack Dempsey, Gene Tunney, and Jack Sharkey were pallbearers at his June 8 funeral. Muldoon was laid to rest in a mausoleum in Kensico Cemetery in Valhalla, NY, near New York Yankees legend Lou Gehrig. His estate was inherited by his secretary Margaret Farrell, whom Muldoon adopted as his daughter.

During his life, Muldoon was a strong advocate for the Boy Scouts of America, citing they were the only organization devoted to leadership-building for young men. On January 3, 1940, Margaret Farrell Muldoon donated 35.9 acres of wooded land owned by William Muldoon to The Bronx Valley Council of the Boys Scouts of America. The land stretched from Old Lake Street to Westchester Avenue, a mile from Muldoon's home and health club, near Rye Lake, and about a mile from Old Orchard Street.

 In 1959, the Boy Scouts sold the land Muldoon donated to them, which had become known as Muldoon Park. In 1978, it was resold to business park developers for $3 million. The sale closed in 1982, and the site eventually became the Starwood building. It is currently part of the property owned by PepsiCo.

7.)STRAUS PARK

Heading down Old Orchard Street, past Cranberry Lake Preserve, is a small, peaceful park. Known as Straus Park, the recreational area at 1571 Old Orchard Street is home to a grassy play area, often used for children's soccer matches. However, years ago, this park had a more sinister reputation.

In the mid-1970s, locals labeled the four-acre park on the boundary between North White Plains and West Harrison a hoodlum haven. Often the site of underage drinking parties, neighbors became concerned if it was a breeding ground for criminal activity.

During a North Castle town meeting in 1974, residents of the quiet community vocalized fear and concern about the people who frequent the park, citing they may be the same people responsible for unreported burglaries. Residents say people at the park may be lurking around the neighborhood and causing trouble.

Straus Park became a focal point for residents in 1974 after a horrible crime in the neighborhood. Around 5 pm one afternoon, a middle-aged man rang the doorbell of a couple's Old Orchard Street home. The man said his car had broken down and asked to borrow a pair of pliers. The friendly homeowner told him to meet him at the garage, which is attached to the house.

However, when the homeowner opened the garage door, he was greeted by two additional men, one of whom was holding a sawed-off shotgun. The burglars ordered the man and his wife to lie face down on their kitchen floor and fired a shot between the man's legs to demonstrate they were serious.

The masked intruders then tied and gagged the couple with nylon stockings, forcing them to lay face-down on their bed. The robbers proceeded to ransack the house, stealing two televisions, jewelry, silverware, an antique gun, a fur coat, and $300 in cash before escaping.

Despite the potential gathering of criminals at Straus Park, the police successfully made the area safe once again. The park was named after Nathan Straus Jr., whose 8-acre property borders Cranberry Lake.

In 1908, while attending Heidelberg University, Nathan Straus Jr. befriended a young Jewish art history scholar from Germany named Otto. He helped him land a job in New York at one of the department store chains his father, Nathan Straus Sr., co-owned, Macy's. A year later, Otto's father passed away, causing him to quit Macy's and return to Germany. Years later, to avoid the severe anti-Semitism of Nazi Germany, Otto and his family enlisted Nathan's help to obtain visas to return to the United States.

Despite Nathan's best efforts, the visas were declined. Ultimately Otto's entire family was interned in Nazi concentration camps. At the end of World War II, he was the only member of his family to survive. In the years that followed, he published the diary of his daughter, Anne

Frank.

Years later, Otto Frank transcribed the diary, which went on to be one of the all-time most well-known books about The Holocaust.

In 1921, Nathan became a member of the New York State Senate. In addition to Macy's, his father co-owned the department store chain Abraham & Straus (remember A&S in The Galleria?). His mother, Helen Sachs Straus, was of the Goldman Sachs family. His brother Peter worked under President Jimmy Carter, owned a radio station, and in 1998 married Marcia Lewis, the mother of Monica Lewinsky.

 Nathan Straus Jr. passed away in 1961. His widow and son, Nathan Straus III, became owners of the estate and, at some time, later sold some of its land to Westchester County, which converted it into Straus Park.

In 2019, the Straus estate was listed for sale with an asking price of $6.75M. The beautiful property features a 14,000-square-foot mansion with 19-foot ceilings. It is on eight acres surrounded by 490 acres of conservation land, including Cranberry Lake.

8.)LOCAL CRIME

The roughly 2.5-mile-long Old Orchard Street is a serene and peaceful suburban street. But, in years past, it had been the site of various strange and eerie crimes.

I

 One of the first eerie crime reports happened back in 1884. That June, newspapers reported that there was an "Insane Man at Large." The menacing story told the tale of a man about 50 years old who escaped from a Brooklyn asylum and had been wandering around the woods between Rye Lake and Old Orchard Street in a semi-nude condition. Brooklyn authorities offered a $50 reward for tips leading to his apprehension. His fate remains unclear.

II

 Around this time, two bandits held up 20-year-old horse and carriage driver John Lynch as he traveled up Old Orchard Street. The bandits robbed and beat Lynch and then returned to their homes in the neighboring Stony Hill community of formerly enslaved people along Buckout Road. Police later identified and arrested the culprits, Thomas Brown and John Jackson, who were sentenced to prison terms at Sing Sing, literally, for highway robbery.

III

A similar crime occurred years later, in 1933. Four masked bandits targeted Harry Acklery, the game warden and sports official. The masked criminals held up Mr. Acklery near the quarry on Old Orchard Street, forcing him from his car and stealing his cash before making a getaway.

IV

In 1942, the police arrested Old Orchard Street resident Stephen Purdy on multiple charges. Mr. Purdy admitted to breaking into his neighbor's Old Orchard Street home earlier in the evening. The victim, A.H. Birdsall, told police that Purdy broke into his home after he jimmied the rear storm door and then busted open a locked drawer. Mr. Purdy maintained despite this, he didn't steal anything. The police also arrested Purdy for stealing an automobile in Yonkers. However, they could not recover the car, which Purdy told police he ditched at The Outers Gun Club on Park Lane.

Park Lane is the street that part of Old Orchard Street turns into near the edge of Woodman's Cove. Park Lane then stretches towards nearby Buckout Road, which partially runs parallel with the central portion of Old Orchard Street, separated by thick woods.

V

In the late summer of 1948, two Harrison police officers responded to a distress call from Viola Van Loan on Old Orchard Street. When patrolmen Charles King and David Agostinelli arrived a few minutes later, they found Mrs. Van Loan sitting on her front lawn laughing and talking to three other ladies. She explained she had been "joking" when she had phoned the police wishing to make an assault charge against her husband, whom the officers determined wasn't even home at the time. She said she merely wanted to see how quickly the police could arrive.

VI

 In 1962, the Jennie Clarkson Home was involved in a bizarre battle with its neighbor, a wholesale egg dealer. The parties engaged in a dispute over whether or not either could put up a fence between the properties. In the 1980s, the Jennie Clarkson Home reported several strange crimes, including one in 1989 when the police received a phone call about a robbery. When they arrived, items from the house had been scattered on the front lawn, but fortunately, the only item reported stolen was a soda can from the kitchen.

VII

An Old Orchard Street resident garnered local fame during the 1960s for his daring jumps out of airplanes. The parachutist made several notable jumps, including one into New York City's Central Park and one where he jumped from 12,500 feet at Westchester County Airport with smoke bombs attached to his boots. He later made local news for choosing to heat his home with a log fire instead of oil.

 Unfortunately, during the 1970s, the police arrested the parachutist for disorderly conduct stemming from a drunken incident where he waved an unloaded rifle at police. Years later, the police arrested him again— this time for driving while intoxicated.

9.) TRAGEDIES

Numerous sad, shocking, and tragic deaths occurred on Old Orchard Street, including an unfortunate automobile accident in 1982.

I

Charles Robinson of nearby Hall Ave died from injuries sustained after his 1970 Volkswagen struck a telephone pole on Old Orchard Street. The 61-year-old White Plains man worked as a letter carrier with the White Plains post office for years and was a deacon at the White Plains Presbyterian Church on North Broadway.

II

Police reported that in 1978, Nils Erikson Jr. and his father, Nils Erikson Sr, attended a family outing near Mr. Erikson's Old Orchard Street home. Around 5:30 pm on December 26, Nils Jr. drove his father home, returned to the family gathering, and then went back to his dad's house around 8 pm. That's when Nils Jr. made an awful discovery.

The Reporter Dispatch reported that after searching the house for his father, Nils Jr. finally found him, nonresponsive, inside a car in the garage. The police determined that he had died from carbon monoxide poisoning. The 81-year-old, born in Sweden in 1897, was predeceased by his wife, Signe, and survived by his son, Nils Jr, and grandson, also named Nils.

III

In 1958, Howard Ulrick of Old Orchard Street had to make an unfortunate phone call to the North Castle Police. Outside his home, he sadly discovered a parked car with its driver slumped over the wheel. The police arrived fast and tried to resuscitate 57-year-old Chappaqua Postmaster James Harrigan but were unsuccessful.

IV

The same year, a 29-year-old Bedford Hills man named Lawrence Brown died at White Plains Hospital from injuries after his pick-up truck collided with a car containing five teenagers near the intersection of Route 22 and Old Orchard Street. The pick-up truck, armed with a snow plow, hit the teenagers' car as it turned from the driveway of the Jennie Clarkson Home.

V

In August 1958, North Castle Police reported the shocking discovery of 31-year-old Mary Collins, found by her husband, suspended in midair from the end of a rope attached to the porch railing of their Old Orchard Street home. Newspapers reported that the police said there was no apparent reason given for the actions of the mother of three but quickly ruled her tragic death a suicide.

VI

In 1957, a bolt of lightning struck and killed a dog owned by a man who lived on Park Lane, which turns into Old Orchard Street. The dog's owner, Joseph, said the lightning burned the chain the dog was tied to in the yard.

VII

In April 1955, Harrison police discovered the body of 43-year-old Old Orchard Street resident Percy Harris in a storage room over the garage of his brother-in-law's house. They told reporters that Mr. Harris had not been in contact with his wife or child for several years, that his mother was critically ill, and that they found a note left for his sister. No one heard the shotgun blast, which left the victim, a World War II veteran, decapitated.

VIII

An unfortunate car accident in 1939 claimed the life of 17-year-old Joseph Pawelski of The Bronx after a car he was riding in with friends sideswiped a telephone pole on Old Orchard Street, resulting in a fatal skull fracture.

IX

In August 1939, in the thick Quarry Heights woods, 500 feet off Old Orchard Street, 85-year-old John Merriman made a gruesome discovery. As he picked berries, his dog began violently barking. At the edge of a 20-foot cliff in a thickly wooded area draped over a rock, the Old Orchard Street resident found a decomposed body.

After further investigation, the police successfully identified the 5'9", 160-pound man as 50-year-old handyman Bruce Graham of Brooklyn, NY.

Detectives discovered a strange collection of his belongings in a clearing seven feet from his corpse. In a pile were two pairs of shoes, two paper bags, a package of razor blades, a near-empty jar of shaving cream, New England road maps, a spoon, a half-gallon bottle of turpentine, a pair of shears, an eyeglass case, a felt hat, two packs of matches, what a spectator declared was "smoke," a potent alcoholic drink, and a mysterious triangular piece of glass.

There were no bloodstains on any of the items, nor did the police find any weapons. Police estimated that Mr. Graham's body had been lying, undiscovered, for the last six weeks.

Mr. Graham's remains were in such a state of decay that Medical Examiner Dr. Squire was not able to perform an autopsy and, therefore, could not determine the precise cause of death. Mr. Graham was buried at the County Cemetery in Valhalla.

10.) ROCKY LEDGE

About a mile south of Straus Park, past the sites of numerous aforementioned tragedies, is a popular gated gravel driveway. For nine months of the year, it is often adorned with a thick chain and a lock. But during the summer months, when the gates are open, it's a whole other world for some.

Since the 1960s, in the summertime, beyond the otherwise nondescript gates surrounded by woods, large crowds have gathered at Old Orchard Street's members-only Rocky Ledge Swimming Association.

The concept for Rocky Ledge began in 1959 when White Plains lawyer Andrew Stevenson gave the local Zoning Board details about a group that wished to build a pool on Old Orchard Street in North White Plains. The proposed site would be on a 13-acre tract opposite the White Plains Reservoir. Mr. Stevenson told the board that his group was reasonably sure of getting water and access rights across land in White Plains to the pool property from the City of White Plains. Despite his positivity, numerous residents opposed the idea for many reasons, including increased traffic and the fear of relying on water from Quarry Heights.

With a membership goal of 500 families at $350 each, the group estimated their pool project would cost about $125,000 for the pool, bathhouse, and other facilities. Despite obstacles, they achieved approval and shortly after, the group that also built the Hilltop

Swimming Pool in Yonkers broke ground on Old Orchard Street.

The pool became the second large construction project in that section of Old Orchard Street, following the recent erection of a nearby fire drill tower. In 1958, the Zoning Board approved plans to build a five-story structure that would be regularly set on fire to help train local fire department recruits.

Throughout the 1970s, the Rocky Ledge Swimming Association grew in popularity, and its swim team won numerous championships and broke multiple records. Unfortunately, around this time, there became a need for an additional landfill in the area, and Old Orchard Street became a possible destination. In 1973, one local politician pitched the idea of dumping non-organic refuse as fill near Rocky Ledge Pool, where a mountain of garbage and landfill could made into a ski run. For whatever reason, the landfill next to the members-only swimming pool gained approval. As that happened, a terrible incident drew local attention.

In April 1975, the New York Police Department conducted a manhunt for murder suspect Michael Richter. The police wanted the 25-year-old Bronx resident for his involvement in the fatal slaying of 19-year-old Robert Jones, who bravely fought back against Richter when he tried to steal his car. Richter also attacked Jones' mother, Mrs. Coreen Jones, who suffered multiple stab wounds from the violent attacker.

A few days after the horrific crime, Harrison police found the stolen 1972 Maverick wrecked and abandoned near the border between Harrison and North White Plains on Park Lane. Two hours later, the

North White Plains police received a phone call.

Mrs. Ann Murchinson, who lived on the estate of Nathan Straus, called the police to report she had spotted a strange man leaving her home. The intruder, who police said proved to be the murder suspect, broke into the house, made a sandwich, and took a glass of milk from the kitchen.

According to police, an attempted burglary in the same general area, on Park Lane, was reported to Harrison police. The events triggered about 50 police officers from Harrison, North Castle, White Plains, and the New York State to comb the wooded area of Old Orchard Street with bloodhounds.

The murder suspect, who, according to police, had a lengthy criminal record including assault and weapon charges, was arrested at about 7 am the following morning at the Rocky Ledge Pool.

The landfill continued to operate in the 1970s in an 800 by 250-foot area neighboring Rocky Ledge Pool. The permit expired in 1976, but since then, the 50-foot-deep sloping site has become subject to garbage dumping by persons unknown.

The news of a potential new landfill next to Rocky Ledge emerged in the 1980s. In 1982, the North Castle Supervisor warned the White Plains Common Council that a planned landfill project could contaminate drinking water in two adjacent reservoirs. Supervisor Lombardi went on to explain that potential significant adverse effects include loss of a functional wetland and associated wildlife habitat, degradation of water quality, shifts in existing drainage patterns in an area that drains into the White Plains water supply and Silver Lake recreational area, and increase in truck traffic through a residential neighborhood.

While multiple politicians valiantly fought against a new landfill, the Rocky Ledge Swim Association fought for it. Their pitch for the landfill also included that it would eventually be capped off and used as a private baseball field for the 125 or so members of the Rocky Ledge Swimming Association, which owns the land. Additionally, they wanted to utilize landfill material, including refuse and tree clippings, to complete the construction of another baseball field and a picnic area and have debris fill in an area of swamp so they could build a tennis court.

A few years later, various headlines made local newspapers, including "Smelly Landfill." A Health Department spokesperson explained that heat and humidity were to blame for the stench at the Rocky Ledge Swimming Association. The odor came from moisture trapped in construction debris dumped at the 3-acre landfill. While she emphasized that the stench poses no danger, multiple landfill neighbors began vocalizing complaints. One neighbor commented, "Sometimes you'll smell it as you come up the hill. It smells like rotten wood or wet cardboard."

Despite the Rocky Ledge Swimming Association fighting to keep the landfill open, it closed again in November 1988 after their permit expired. The president of Rocky Ledge Swimming Association, Pat Lee, told reporters they'd be taking steps to cap the landfill as soon as possible after multiple locals complained about illegal dumping. At its closure, the landfill was at two-thirds of its 275,000-ton capacity.

Shortly after, the New York State Department of Environmental Conservation ordered the landfill operator, Jub Development Corp, to cap it. Jub never complied with the order, and subsequently, the company's owner was sent to prison on an unrelated charge.

Despite numerous lawsuits and complaints of stinky smells, patrons happily frequented their local members-only swimming club, often paying upwards of $600 per family per year to belong.

Recurring special events at Rocky Ledge have included an annual Jump Rope Contest and a $25 premium event, "Italian Night." Per their flyer, the BYOB event features sausage & peppers, soda, coffee, tea, and a DJ, sponsored by "The Mansion on Broadway" (formerly a Knights of Columbus hall). A former teaching assistant and pool member described it as "one of the best places to see and be seen." Around this time, a local police department began operating a shooting range a few yards from the pool.

Starting in 2010, Rocky Ledge became home to a popular spooky walk-through attraction on weekends leading up to Halloween. The organizers of The Haunt previously operated numerous local scary attractions, including "The Haunted Dead End" and the famous White Plains Zombie Walk, where folks dress up as zombies and stroll together through downtown White Plains.

On peak nights since opening, The Haunt would draw several hundred patrons paying at least $25 each to walk through its haunted attractions, including a spooky cornfield and a scary, haunted walk through the woods.

The Haunt successfully operated for over a decade. Its location at Rocky Ledge was perhaps ironic to some locals, as the "scary walk through the woods", populated with make-believe monsters, witches, and Dracula actually borders Buckout Road, the street infamously dubbed as "America's scariest street," the subject of several books and a horror movie starring Danny Glover.

In 2022, after about 60 years in business, the once-exclusive Rocky Ledge pool announced its closure following the news that the New York Attorney General had filed a lawsuit against the Rocky Ledge Swimming Association for fraud.

11.) WHITE PLAINS RESERVOIR

Adjacent to the site of the former Rocky Ledge pool, police shooting range, fire training facility, and the former landfill is White Plains Reservoir. Small compared to the much larger nearby Kensico Reservoir, the water supply built in 1900 provides a nice scenic background on one side of a small stretch of Old Orchard Street.

The White Plains Reservoir made news in the summer of 1923 after the arrest of a millionaire baker's son named Walter S. Ward. The police charged him with fatally shooting a 19-year-old sailor from Haverhill, MA, named Clarence Peters.

Allegedly, rather than being dumped, the 32-year-old killer who attended Yale University carefully laid his victim's body on the ground. Peter's bloody body was found a day later by two telephone linemen near the reservoir.

The discovery of Peters' body at first attracted little attention. Investigators initially believed the incident to be a bootlegger's feud, and for several days, the body remained unidentified. Additional confusion arose as some newspapers reported that the terrible incident had occurred at the nearby Kensico Reservoir.

After the police identified the body, Walter Ward and his attorney walked into the sheriff's office and announced in a formal statement that he had shot Peters in self-defense. Walter's father, George Ward, was the president of the Ward Baking Company and vice president of the Brooklyn Tip-Tops, a Federal League baseball club. Walter alleged that Clarence Peters was amongst blackmailers who demanded vast sums of money from him.

Despite Ward admitting to the crime, the trial began 484 days later. Walter's trial ended with his acquittal, and he walked away a free man.

Before a barbed wire fence ran along the reservoir's edge, the area was a popular destination for hikers and nature lovers. Old-time log roads and walking trails wandered through the hilly, rocky sectors of the watershed's lands, decorated with maple, sycamore, and spruce trees.

The 469-acre watershed also includes two small lakes in addition to the reservoir, which are used if there's overflow, like when winter snow melts. During the 1960s, the land was popular for walks, fishing, camping, picnicking, and quiet meditation.

During the 1970s, the White Plains Reservoir and its smaller Reservoir #2 were abandoned after city officials discovered shrimp and several types of algae in the water supply. The shocking discovery led to the installation of one of the region's largest micro filters. The $330,000 project in 1981 eventually led to the city of White Plains utilizing the reservoirs again, taking around 3 million gallons of water daily. During this time, Rocky Ledge fought to have a landfill adjacent to the reservoir on their property.

In July 1984, police divers frantically combed the 35-foot-deep reservoir, searching for a drowning victim. 18-year-old Michael O'Connor and two of his teenage friends visited the site that day around 3 pm. One of the friends told police, "We were out by the rock. He said he would stay at the dam and get some sun. The next thing we knew, he removed his pants and entered the water. We saw him splashing around, and then he was gone. His pants are still on the dam." After eight days of multiple diving expeditions, police divers recovered the victim's body.

The tragic incident invoked a surprising response from residents: complaints. Residents demanded more public swimming pools, citing the only nearby ones available are at Gardella and Kittrell parks, which are both near apartment complexes and, therefore, typically crowded. The Saxon Woods swimming pool on Mamamaroneck Ave is open to the entire county and consequently always falls during summer days. One letter to a local newspaper even mentioned a former pool at George Washington Elementary School on Orchard Street that had closed sometime during the late 1970s due to fiscal constraints.

Years later, the traffic bureau erected a new sign near the reservoir's "No Swimming" signage. The sign warns motorists to be careful of turtle crossing. In the spring months, a population of turtles, sometimes mating, are frequently seen crossing Old Orchard Street. In 2018, someone stole the sign.

12.) THE SHOPPING CENTER

Old Orchard Street ends at its intersection with Orchard Street in front of White Plains Reservoir #2. At that point, the street turns into Reservoir Road, a short, roughly 0.2-mile-long street ending in a famous neighborhood shopping center.

The North White Plains Shopping Center is currently anchored by a massive Super Stop & Shop grocery store and the popular Abatino's Pizzeria, home of its locally well-known "Chop-Chop Salad." Before the late 1990s, however, the shopping center had a different look and was the site of multiple newsworthy incidents.

The area of the shopping center used to be a swamp. Its stores were built on piles ranging from 60 to 100 feet deep into swamp muck for foundation. As far back as the 1960s, stores in the shopping center suffered from sinking.

In 1960, the anchor store of North White Shopping Center was a 22,500 sq. ft. First National Store, known locally as Finast. That summer, foundation experts drove steel pilings underneath the popular grocery store to help combat it suffering from sinking 16 inches since opening just a few years prior.

People connected to the venture have been reluctant to discuss the cause of the sinking. Locals pointed out that the swamplands were a popular dumping destination for gigantic truck-size tree stumps and concrete. Speculation is that when wooden pilings were first sunk for the building, the debris gave strong resistance, later subsiding slowly.

A row of shops near Finast included a hair salon, Kavish's Pharmacy, and Koven's Deli. In 1966, a bandit robbed the shopping center's B and B Spirit Shop at gunpoint. The robber was a young, Black man in his 20s who wore sunglasses, a dark raincoat, and a brown felt hat. He entered the liquor store around 7:30 pm and asked for a bottle of wine. When he was told that the store didn't carry the brand he was looking for, he paid 50 cents for a substitute. While the clerk was ringing up the sale, the man pulled out a gun and ordered the clerk to fill a bag with cash. He then backed out of the store and ran across the parking area. The police issued a 13-state alarm for the armed robber.

In March 1987, the liquor store was burglarized once again. Between 9 pm on a Thursday and 9 am the next day, the thief made a hole through the roof of B and B Spirits, then punched a hole through the sheetrock wall to access the store. Once inside, the burglar stole money from the store's office. After that, the thief broke into Abatino's restaurant next door, but nothing was reported as stolen.

It's unclear whether the police apprehended the B and B Spirits burglars or why they targeted the store. The liquor store's owner, John Balog, was a longtime Westchester resident who served in the US Army during World War II. He saw action in the Pacific Theatre, reached the rank of Master Sergeant, and later became a chapter

Commander of The Disabled American War Veterans.

 In 1983, an armed robber held up the shopping center's bank, Village Savings. Police said the criminal walked up to a glass-enclosed teller's booth and held a small automatic handgun on the ledge of the teller's booth. The 5'8" White man in his late 30s then handed the teller a camera bag over the top of the booth and ordered her to fill the bag with money. The robber walked out of the bank with a bag full of cash. He then ran up Reservoir Road towards Old Orchard Street.

 Years later, Village Savings closed, and First Fidelity became the shopping center's new bank. One afternoon in August 1995, a criminal entered the bank and shouted, "This is a robbery! Give me your 100s and 50s!" The robber showed bank tellers a brown-paper package and told them it was a bomb that would explode in three minutes. The robber, described as a 5'8" White man in his late 30s or early 40s, walked out of the bank and ran up Reservoir Road toward Old Orchard Street. Fortunately, the bomb squad found no explosives and discovered the "bomb" was a cement brick wrapped in brown paper with masking tape and a piece of antenna sticking out.

 Over the years, various stores have come and gone from the shopping center. When Koven's Deli left, P&P Delicatessen took its place beside Judi Stein's Embassy 5&10. In 1992, Kadish Pharmacy made the news after a burglar busted in and stole a large amount of prescription drugs. In 1995, Dayna's Hallmark made headlines for selling a $10 million winning lottery ticket. But, of all the stores in the shopping center, the most memorable is perhaps the iconic red building in back, Handleman's.

Handleman's Garden Center was the shopping center's original store, dating back to 1940. Known for its popular holiday displays, Handleman's sold various things, including plants, fresh apples, cider, pumpkins, decorations, Christmas trees, and garden supplies.

In 1958, a robber broke into the store after hours and busted into the safe. He stole $2,700 in cash and checks but left behind a vital clue. The police found a scrap of paper with the suspect's name and address in White Plains. The police eventually tracked the 19-year-old thief to Ann Arbor, MI, where they arrested him.

In 1979, Handleman's iconic red building was engulfed by one of the most dangerous and memorable fires in the area's history. The flames were as high as 250 feet, turning the store into a glowing inferno. Despite the bravery of firefighters from six nearby departments, the blaze destroyed the 40-year-old structure in less than an hour. The nursery building was nothing but charred rubble.

Years later, firefighters at the scene commented that if this fire had happened today, it would have been a significant Hazmat incident with all the pesticides and fertilizers. Fortunately, no injuries occurred. Handleman's eventually rebuilt and reopened.

The popular nursery is perhaps most remembered for its iconic holiday walk-through displays. Ahead of the times, Handleman's offered its annual Christmas Wonderland. Described as the most beautiful and largest Christmas display in Westchester County, the walk-through featured numerous large animatronics, live characters, an interactive enchanted snow forest, a petting zoo, and the opportunity for guests to meet Santa Claus.

Handleman's became the first in the area to have a walk-through Easter display complete with animatronics and a chance to meet The Easter Bunny. Perhaps its most iconic, though, was its annual Halloween Horror. The haunted attraction was the first in the area and grew so popular that school trips from throughout the county attended. Featuring giant animatronics, including a massive Frankenstein's Monster, and various live actors, including the legendary Wanda the Witch, Handleman's became the place to celebrate the Halloween season.

While Handleman's was a major draw for patrons to the shopping center, Finast was the anchor store. Throughout the 1970s and 1980s, it was one of two supermarkets in the neighborhood. The other, an A&P around the corner on North Broadway (now a CVS), and Finast were both fined in 1977 for selling merchandise past its expiration dates.

In late April 1980, local police found a sketchy Ford van parked outside the Finast after hours. Upon investigating, they found two New York City men sleeping in the vehicle, which not only turned out to be stolen but also had loads of stolen property and burglar's tools. The van's occupants, two guys in their 40s, one of whom was hiding a hacksaw inside his coat, were arrested with bail set at $50,000.

In January 1988, a man walked into the bookkeeper's office of Finast around 8:30 pm, pulled out a handgun, and demanded money. The bookkeeper handed him money, which the robber stuffed into a shopping bag before bolting out of the store.

Around a year later, Finast was renamed Edwards, while Handleman's was transformed into a regional nursery chain store called Arcadian. Eventually, in 1996, the supermarket's parent company, based in Connecticut, suggested demolishing the supermarket and other nearby shops within The North White Plains Shopping Center, replacing it with a proposed Super Stop & Shop covering an area of 47,650 square feet.

In the late 1990s, demolition crews took down stores such as Arcadian and Embassy 5&10. The shopping center's parking lot underwent a major renovation. Within a year, the new, massive Super Stop & Shop triumphantly opened its doors.

The supermarket is massive and even has a robot named Marty patrolling its aisles. Despite the store's expansion, it is still possible to see and smell the vast neighboring marshland and swamp from its entrance, which used to be connected to the shopping center's ground.

A few months after the opening of Super Stop & Shop, a gigantic brush fire broke out at the neighboring marshland. The blaze began in the early afternoon between George Washington School and the supermarket and raged until 11 pm the following evening. Units from White Plains and North White Plains extinguished the fire and successfully prevented injuries or property loss.

13.) THE EXPLOSION

George Washington Elementary School on Orchard Street is located right off I-287's Exit 7A. The exit ramp puts cars on the Central Westchester Parkway for about two blocks, passing under the Grant Avenue overpass before exiting between Grant Ave and GW School on Beech Street. In 1994, that overpass was destroyed in an explosion.

Named after former U.S. president Ulysses S. Grant, Grant Avenue was built in 1892 and runs parallel to Clinton Street, which was initially built in 1870 and named after New York's first governor, George Clinton. Both residential streets are off of North Broadway and just a few blocks away from George Washington School, over the Grant Avenue overpass.

Shortly past midnight on a clear, 71-degree summer night on Wednesday, July 27, 1994, a propane gas truck traveling eastbound on I-287 slammed into the overpass at Grant Ave, shearing off a supporting column, exploding, and launching a massive fireball into a White Plains residential neighborhood.

The crash created a thunderous booming noise that immediately woke much of the neighborhood. Some people thought there was an earthquake or that a bomb had dropped.

A local policeman who lived in the neighborhood commented to *The Reporter Dispatch*, "It was like daylight. It rumbled like thunder. It flashed like lightning. But then it didn't darken. I've never seen anything like it in my life. I looked out the back windows. You could see the grass. Everything. I thought downtown White Plains blew up."

A man on nearby North Kensico Ave reported hearing screeching tires. "I've lived here all my life, and I knew it was a tractor-trailer, and I knew he was going to hit someone. Then I saw a ball of flames, just like in the movies."

The boom awoke brave 14-year-old George Washington School and Cub Scout Pack 1 alumni Jared Heyde, who, along with his dad Fred, went to investigate. Mr. Heyde commented to reporters, "My son thought it was a nuclear explosion. He came running down the stairs. We drove around looking for it, and it was just right here. It's scary. Basically, it looked like a plane crash because there were so many flames around."

Around 12:28 am, the White Plains police department received numerous 911 telephone reports about an explosion and house fires erupting on Grant Avenue, Lennox Avenue, and Clinton Street.

The enormous blast killed the truck driver instantly and sent firefighters scrambling to help injured victims on Grant Ave and Clinton Street. The disaster caused sparking downed wires, flaming trees, and burning homes, including one which the fireball wholly destroyed. Despite about 23 people suffering injuries, area residents, firefighters, and ambulance crews worked together to prevent any additional loss of human life.

Hours after the explosion, ashes were still falling, and residents were discovering further damage. The Grant Ave bridge had buckled, the pavement scorched, and a nearby chain-link fence melted. A family who had recently moved to Clinton Street off North Broadway from Sri Lanka discovered the truck's undercarriage smashed into their garage.

The police found the burned body of 23-year-old truck driver Peter Conway in a ditch. His massive truck was 62 feet long and 8 feet wide with a combined weight of vehicle and cargo of 80,160 pounds. He was hauling 9,200 gallons of liquid propane for the Paracoe Fuel Corporation of Smithtown, NY. After the tank hit a column of the Grant Ave overpass, the front head of the tank fractured, releasing the propane, which vaporized into gas and ignited.

According to reports conducted during an investigation after the tragic incident, Mr. Conway's truck had broken down on I-287 just two days before the crash due to a drive shaft problem.

The investigation also revealed that in the 80 days before the accident, the two drivers who shared the truck for deliveries made 37 false entries, 25 of which were made by Mr. Conway. For example, on several occasions, one of the two drivers had listed himself as being off duty for 24 to 48 hours, during which he was actually on duty, making pickups at refineries, and not sleeping as required.

On the night of the crash, at around 12:30, the driver of a vehicle about 1/4 mile behind Mr. Conway's truck observed him driving approximately 55 to 60 miles per hour in the center lane. The witness stated that the truck "drifted" from the center lane across the left lane and onto the shoulder, striking the median guardrail. He said he saw no signals or brake lights during this movement.

In addition to injuries sustained by 19 residents and four firefighters were the casualties of a flock of birds. A woman on Grant Ave said a man kept chickens and pigeons in his home, and "now they're all over the front yard, dead."

The Grant Avenue overpass remained closed to vehicles for several years before reopening as a one-way street. After nearly two decades, the overpass reopened as a two-way street connecting Grant Avenue to Beech Street near George Washington School.

14.) THE NORTH WHITE PLAINS TRAIN STATION

The North White Plains train station is located off North Broadway, less than a mile from the Grant Avenue explosion site. The station is situated on Fisher Avenue, approximately half a mile away from the North White Plains Shopping Center and Orchard Street. Interestingly, when first constructed in 1735, Orchard Street was initially named Fisher Place.

When introduced in 1972, the North White Plains train station served as a replacement for the former New York Central Railroad-built Holland Avenue station, a low-level northbound-only side platform located near the south end of the current station, near the tunnel. Once Penn Central dissolved in 1976, Contrail took responsibility for commuter service until the Metropolitan Transportation Authority established Metro-North-Railroad in 1983.

The trains departing North White Plains can transport commuters south to New York City's Grand Central Station in about 40 minutes or northbound just past Brewster in Putnam County, NY, in about 50 minutes. While the train station provides a major convenience to the neighborhood, it's also been the site of numerous horrific events dating back to 1910 when a train struck and killed Civil War veteran Samuel Palmer.

II

In 1910, a nightly freight train used to run between North White Plains and Melrose Junction. On the evening of October 13, the rear brakeman, Edgar M. Hogan, stepped down from the rear end of the train as it was about to make its delivery run to Melrose.

As a 22-year veteran of the railroad, Hogan always carried a lantern while crossing the tracks. He would then place the lantern back on the platform of the train car. Unfortunately, on this night, a northbound local train quietly approached and didn't see Mr. Hogan, who had just straddled the electrified third rail of the train tracks. The train struck him, knocking him against the electrified rail, causing instant death.

III

The police raided the North White Plains train yard about an hour past midnight late one night in June 1949. They arrested seven hobos who had turned the area around the train station into their makeshift homes. All the men pleaded guilty to the charges and received a 30-day jail sentence. An eighth vagrant, however, managed to escape the police.

A subsequent police raid led to the arrest of ten men, who they found sleeping in freight cars at the NWP station. This time, the court sentenced each vagrant to 60 days at Westchester County Jail.

IV

On Thursday morning, January 2, 1975, a New York City-bound passenger train that began its route in North White Plains departed the NWP Station at 7:57 am. As the train approached the Bronx Botanical Garden station around 8:14 am, the conductor apparently ignored a warning signal.

The train plowed into the rear of a New York City-bound train from Hartsdale, derailing four of its cars. Passengers in both trains, their faces buried in newspapers or magazines, were suddenly jolted out of their seats. 232 people suffered injuries, primarily facial cuts and broken noses. The two trains carried 1,400 to 1,600 passengers, and railroad officials said it was fortunate there had not been more injuries.

V

Shortly after 6 pm on Saturday, December 17, 1977, police at the North White Plains train station arrested a rowdy man with a loaded gun.

Witnesses said the incident began when 39-year-old Bronx man Charles Chartier took a rifle from a brown paper bag and started to load it while the train was between Brewster and White Plains as it headed to New York City. Two passengers pounced on Charles and wrestled the gun away from him. A scuffle ensued. The train's conductor made an emergency stop in North White Plains, where the police took Charles into custody. It's unclear what the gunman's intentions were or the names of the heroic passengers who may have prevented a terrible tragedy.

VI

On the morning of July 13, 1978, at North White Plains station, eleven people were injured when a passenger train was hit from the back by an empty train. At 6:45 am, the empty train that was moving cars from the western yard of the station to the eastern yard collided with the Manhattan-bound commuter train, causing five out of its eight cars to derail. The injured passengers were immediately taken to White Plains Hospital.

Later that day, investigators from five state and federal safety and railroad agencies swarmed the North White Plains train yard to find out what happened. One investigator revealed that a brakeman was not in the lead car that hit the stationary train, which had boarded its passengers a few minutes before the crash. If this were the case, then the engineer would not have been aware of the second train's position in the station.

VII

In late August 1981, three teenagers from Greenburgh boarded the 11:30 pm train out of Grand Central Station. After the train pulled out of the White Plains station, the trio changed cars, moving to one with only four other passengers and a conductor.

One of the teens then approached the conductor and said, "Don't move. Don't say nothing," as he held a gun to the trainman's head. The bandit took the conductor's belt pouch, containing ticket money collected on the train and his own money.

The trio, described as Black youths wearing jeans, plaid shirts, and white sneakers, each displayed firearms as they worked their way down the train car, taking money, credit cards, and a watch from commuters.

About five minutes after departing from the White Plains station, the train reached North White Plains. As the robbers approached the last two people in the car, the electric-powered train's automatic doors slid open. The gunman who held up the conductor tripped while jumping out of the train, dropping his gun, which discharged as it hit the ground. The 17-year-old gunman recovered the weapon, fired two warning shots into the air from the platform, and then fled with the others.

Detectives tracked the three robbers, two of whom are brothers, to their respective homes in Greenburgh, where they were arrested. Three weeks prior, the train robbers had been arrested for robbing a Good Humor ice cream truck.

VIII

In late 1983, the police arrested a Bronx man at the North White Plains train station after being tipped off that he was carrying a pillowcase filled with silverware stolen from a house in Goldens Bridge. The bandit pleaded guilty to the charges.

IX

In February 1994, a White Plains man pleaded guilty to raping a female jogger on a trail near the North White Plains train station. The barbaric knife-point attack occurred in October 1993 in a county park bordering the Bronx River Parkway, adjacent to the train station, near Fisher Lane.

The 22-year-old victim was jogging on the bicycle path when a man with a knife attacked her at about 5:30 pm. A half-hour later, the police arrested the 20-year-old attacker and charged him with robbery and first-degree rape. He was sentenced to prison and paroled in 2010.

X

A bizarre attacker ambushed a 56-year-old man a few moments after he parked his car at the North White Plains train station commuter parking lot. At around 7 am on Friday, September 27, while walking towards the train station, an unknown attacker came up behind him and hit him twice in the back of the head with a tire iron. The attacker ran off without saying or stealing anything.

XI

In January 2001, a tow truck assisted a snow-bound vehicle stuck at a railroad crossing at nearby Virginia Road. As the tow truck driver attempted to extricate the car, the cantilever arms came down on the truck as the warning bells rang. Moments later, a southbound train that had just left North White Plains collided with the car at 60 mph, splitting the tow truck in half.

 The collision damaged the train and scattered debris across the tracks and street. A crane was needed to lift the mangled wrecker onto a flatbed truck. Luckily, there were no injuries.

XII

North White Plains is the 14th busiest station in Westchester, with about 2,500 daily riders. In June 2005, torrential rain led to massive flooding, which left over 200 cars at the train station's outdoor parking lot submerged to their hoods.

The need for indoor parking became abundantly clear, and within a few years, a new five-story, 186,000-square-foot parking garage opened. The new pre-cast concrete and brick structure fronts Haarlem Avenue and Bond Street near the train station. It provides 500 parking spots and has 1,000 square feet of retail space on its ground floor.

 In 2016, the blockbuster thriller *The Girl on the Train*, with a loaded cast including Emily Blunt, Lisa Kudrow, and Laura Prepon, filmed scenes on the Fisher Ave bridge next to the North White Plains train station, across the tracks from the parking garage.

XIII

In late October 2018, two Metro-North Railroad employees sustained injuries after one of their cars parked at the train yard exploded. The owner of the exploded car, Gerald Shroeder, reportedly was storing propane tanks in it.

 The car completely blew apart and left debris scattered around the parking lot. Sadly, a few weeks later, in early December, Mr. Schroeder passed away.

15.) DINERS

Westchester County is home to many popular privately owned diners throughout its many localities, and North White Plains is no exception. The Townhouse Diner on North Broadway, around the corner from Old Orchard Street, is very well-liked by locals. However, many may be unaware that North White Plains used to have a second diner, and the location of the neighborhood's original 24-hour joint may surprise you.

The Terminal Diner opened several decades ago off North Broadway on Fisher Lane in the North White Plains train yard. Its logical location made it a perfect stop for locals and rail riders. Throughout the years, though, it was the site of numerous incidents, starting shortly after opening its doors.

In February 1950, sanitation inspector William Scoralick filed a complaint against the diner's owner, Canio Nannariello. In early March, Mr. Nannariello pleaded guilty to violating the Westchester sanitary code for operating an eating establishment without obtaining a permit.

Before the year ended, another White Plains resident, Vito De Cosmo, became the owner of the Terminal Diner. This information became public knowledge on December 7, 1950, when Mr. De Cosmo filed a complaint with the police stating that between 12:15 and 3 am, someone at the diner stole his Moroccan leather wallet containing $152.

By 1952, the diner was again featured in local newspapers after its new operator, Jack Cooper, filed a complaint against two 20-something-year-old customers for storming into the kitchen, throwing food around, and using obscene language.

A year later, a woman reported that her gold watch had gone missing while at the diner, which had now been rebranded as Bill's Terminal Diner.

Traditionally, the diner owners have paid only nominal rent to the railroad. In return for this consideration, the owners have agreed to remain open on a 24-hour basis so that train crews and road workers would have a place to eat.

In the mid-1950s, a new owner named John Gendron took over The Terminal Diner. Unfortunately, he was welcomed with a minor annoyance when a thief stole his overcoat and hat from the diner's clothes rack. However, Mr. Gendron didn't let that discourage him. He worked hard and took the establishment to new heights in popularity.

By the late 1960s, Mr. Gendron had purchased the land where the diner was located. He kept the diner open 24 hours daily and due to his efforts, the diner suffered fewer issues with stolen property.

Shockingly, in 1965, the police arrested one of the diner's short-order cooks for his involvement in an illegal gambling ring. The police believed the operation grossed about $88 million yearly from unlawful bets on horses, sports, and lotteries.

Old-timers recall the diner's one-story stucco building featured old double-hung wooden windows, a tile floor, a fireplace, and an early 1900s telephone booth. The cozy eatery had three booths and a counter with fifteen stools.

Coffee would be served in old-fashioned earthenware mugs from large coffee urns seasoned for decades to give the locally famous coffee its character. Freshly baked pastries were proudly displayed in an old-fashioned glass case near a shuffle alley bowling game.

Presiding over the late-night crowd of workers and folks stopping in to sober up after patronizing a local bar was Steve Markacs. Known for his locally famous cheeseburgers and gravy fries, Steve ran away from his Pennsylvania home when he was just 14.

Steve's colorful resume includes working as a lumberjack and as a gandy dancer driving spikes on the railroad. He has worked in a circus, in Death Valley, mining borax, and twice at a carnival sideshow. Steve loved interacting with the diner patrons, and amongst his favorites was World Series champion New York Yankees third baseman Clete Boyer.

In 1969, the police arrested Steve, who was 52 at the time, for his alleged involvement in promoting gambling and possession of policy play records. It's unclear whether anything became of this or if the police had made a mistake.

During the 1970s, the diner was torn down and rebuilt about 100 yards from its original location. The new building, made of chrome, glass, and stainless steel, looked very different than its original building but still had food that its legions of customers raved about. As the diner was off North Broadway, it opened under the punny name, The Off-Broadway Diner.

In March 1975, a man sat at the Off-Broadway Diner counter, ate breakfast, and waited for some customers to leave. He then pointed a gun at the diner's cook, Gus, and shouted, "This is a stick up!" The gunman then forced Gus and a diner customer onto the kitchen floor, robbing them and the register of cash before fleeing.

Just two years later, late at night, around 1:30 am, a 6-foot-tall masked man in dark clothing entered the diner. When the bandit failed to open the cash register with a knife, he pointed a handgun at Gus, who was working behind the counter. The bandit instead robbed Gus of $25 and fled.

Despite being destroyed in the early 1980s, many old school residents still have fond memories of the neighborhood joint that many affectionately referred to as "The Cheese Diner," as it was apparently where local police officers would pick up cheese sandwiches for jail inmates.

Luckily for locals, another diner is just a half mile up the road on North Broadway. Just past the intersection of Reservoir Road and North Broadway, next to what is now a Mexican restaurant that was formerly an Asian restaurant and, before that, a German beer hall called Maxl's, is a popular local eatery that has also gone through a variety of names.

In the mid-1950s, the Castle Hill Diner on North Broadway had numerous incidents, including when four young men from White Plains got into an altercation with the diner's owner, resulting in an actual food fight. The owner called the police to report that the juveniles threw hamburgers and fries around the restaurant. Unfortunately, the bizarre rumpus caused the diner's owner, Mr. Olivia, to seek medical condition due to his heart condition.

Thursday, November 2, 1961, marked the grand opening of the brand-new Sherwood Diner. Located at 720 North Broadway, the newly built restaurant celebrated its grand opening by giving away balloons, key chains, and a special door prize: a 19" portable Zenith television! The diner's owners also operated The Hartsdale Diner on Central Avenue, next to the firehouse.

By 1977, the Sherwood Diner had changed ownership and became the North Castle Diner. It made headlines relatively quickly after the police arrested a Connecticut car thief covered in mud while eating breakfast at the counter.

In April 1983, armed robbers attacked 29-year-old gasoline truck driver Thomas Manuel while making a 2 am delivery to the Presto Service Station on 780 North Broadway. A man with a pistol approached Thomas while another man snuck up and handcuffed him before tying him to a nearby vent pipe with a rope.

The robbers then drove away in the truck, which the police later found, emptied of its 6,300-gallon load across the Tappan Zee Bridge in Nanuet. Still handcuffed, Thomas managed to break free from the vent and make it to the nearby North Castle Diner to report the theft.

Other police incidents over the years have included the police recovering a stolen car from the diner parking lot after receiving a tip from a patron that a suspicious 1978 Pontiac had been parked there for several days. Another time, the police arrested a man under investigation for felony tax evasion at the diner after he accepted a bribe.

In the 1990s, the police arrested a woman at the diner after she allegedly used profanity and abusive language towards the diner staff. Oddly, the very same day, news broke that the restaurant had been penalized for multiple health violations.

The violations included:
- The storage of ammonia in the dishwashing area.
- Improper reheating of potentially hazardous foods in a steam table.
- Food left at improper temperatures.

Some old-timers recall being served omelets that sometimes included pieces of wire the diner staff would chalk up to pieces of a brush used while cooking.

After sitting idle for several years, new owners purchased the North Castle Diner and reopened it as the freshly revamped Townhouse Diner. The popular restaurant made headlines in February 2024 for what looked like an FBI raid.

Fortunately, the considerable commotion of police cars and government agents in the Townhouse Diner parking lot was also accompanied by a film crew from Dick Wolf's hit crime series *FBI: Most Wanted*. The Emmy-nominated CBS drama starring Alexa Davalos and Dylan McDermott filmed several scenes at the diner for an episode of season 5, including one where a gunman on a motorcycle fatally shoots two FBI agents.

16.) THE GRETNA GREEN INN

A century ago, long before popular local eateries on North Broadway like Sir John's Plaza and Pee Wee's, later The Little Spot, existed, there was a notorious local two-story establishment marked with a large "DINING DANCING" sign facing North Broadway. Situated near the former North White Plains School was The Gretna Green Inn, a rumored mob-run speakeasy.

The venue had a restaurant on its ground floor, while the upper floor featured a dance floor. It was 1930, during the prohibition era in the United States, when the making, selling, or transportation of alcoholic beverages were considered illegal. Rumors persisted that the Gretna Green Inn violated the no-liquor law and it became the subject of an undercover investigation.

After undercover agents unsuccessfully tried to shut down the establishment, about 50 North White Plains residents signed a petition declaring The Gretna Green Inn a public nuisance. While residents couldn't say for sure what was happening inside its doors, there were rumors of shadowy underworld figures conducting shady business amongst a liquor-consuming crowd of mobsters and sketchy showgirls.

The petition led to a court proceeding. Inside the crowded courtroom, packed with various shadowy figures and nightlife regulars, including Snowy Winters, a gal who is said to be able to consume 50 drinks in a sitting, the jury refused to convict.

A year later, in March 1931, the police reported that someone pumped Gretna Green regular Lawrence Volpie, aka "Big Bob Mason," with 13 bullets during a poker game at the North White Plains establishment.

Half a dozen gangsters allegedly were involved in some part of the fatal gunfight, and police held eleven people as material witnesses. Autopsy photos showed the victim, a veteran of World War I and a former prizefighting boxer, had dark wounds, cauliflower ears, and a tattoo of a long-haired woman. On his body, the police found a watch bearing the inscription "To Bob from L. Pope 10-7-30."

While a motive remained unclear, Westchester authorities said that Mason was "the right-hand man of the biggest racketeer in Westchester." Many believe this referenced alleged mob bootlegger Louie Pope.

Mr. Pope and "Big Bob Mason" operated the Central Hotel on Liberty Square in Port Chester. The popular establishment was known for its long bar and regular live Hawaiian band. The pair was frequently seen hanging out together at the Gretna Green Inn.

Mr. Pope lived in a lavish White Plains mansion on Gedney Park Drive, rumored to have had a tunnel built in the basement as an escape route should federal agents strike. Authorities believed he was responsible for transporting and selling thousands of cases of booze to Westchester speakeasies in addition to running a gas fraud scheme. Despite the rumors, Mr. Pope was never convicted of any crimes.

The infamous fatal North White Plains shooting involving well-known personalities of the underworld led detectives to search for two men wanted in connection to the murder who fled the scene: a cab driver named James Raimo and a man described as a Brooklyn gangster going by the alias Bucky O'Neill.

After a police search of almost a year, Bucky O'Neill and another James Raimo surrendered to face the indictment. While in custody, Raimo exhibited signs of tuberculosis and was transferred to Grasslands Hospital. Both suspects posted bail and were released.

After seven years, the murder case against Bucky O'Neill and James Raimo was finally brought to trial at the Westchester County Courthouse in White Plains. In 1939, the jury of six men and six women heard testimony from numerous individuals, including "Gene the Barber" and "Markus Marks," often including phrases such as "I can't recall" and "I don't remember." The jury took the case at noon and returned their verdict at 4:15 pm: not guilty.

Despite the court not convicting anyone of the murder of "Big Bob Mason," the Gretna Green Inn was successfully shut down. It's believed the location of the infamous roadhouse on North Broadway became the site of Oscar's Tavern and later a professional building next to a gas station.

17.) REVOLUTIONARY WAR HEADQUARTERS

The neighborhood takes pride in the fact that General George Washington stayed here numerous times during the Revolutionary War—so much so that the neighborhood elementary school on Orchard Street was even named in his honor. However, the precise location of General Washington's headquarters has become the topic of controversy as two different historically significant houses in the neighborhood have both staked their claim as Washington's Headquarters.

Less than 1.5 miles from George Washington School is the Elijah Miller House on Virginia Road. The 18th-century North White Plains house originally stood on a 600-acre farm. The historic home is said to have been occupied by General Washington three times during the Revolutionary War:

1. October 1776
2. During the summer of 1778.
3. During the summer of 1781,

The home was owned by Elijah Miller, who died in August 1776 while serving in the Westchester Militia in battle. His widow, Anne, hosted Washington during his visits during the Revolutionary War as the United States tried to gain independence from England.

47-year-old British general William Howe led General Washington's opposition. General Howe's redcoat army had been chasing Washington's troops through Brooklyn and Manhattan during the summer of 1776 before reaching Westchester County that October.

In late October 1776, General Washington envisioned a way to stop Howe's army. He found the place for the ultimate in strategic retreats: a crescent of rocky hills surrounding an impassable swamp, North White Plains. Adjacent to the Elijah Miller House in North White Plains was the high Miller Hill, essentially above and behind what is now the Dunkin Donuts that neighbors a small cemetery on North Broadway.

When the Revolution began, Washington was 44 years old. He stood over 6 feet tall, weighed 190 pounds, and was a superb horseman and a natural athlete. It's said that he could ride in the saddle all day supervising his troops and then return to the Elijah Miller House and spend hours at his desk writing dispatches, getting only three or four hours of sleep per night.

Across from Miller Hill is another large slope off North Broadway overlooking Old Orchard Street, known locally as Mount Misery. While Washington's troops referred to the steep hill on present-day Nethermont Ave by its miserable nickname because they braved the rain and cold while preparing defenses, awaiting a British attack, some local historians believe the name has a darker origin.

It's believed that the Native Americans, the Siwanoy, who resided in the area before colonization, had a large fort on the steep hill, offering views of the valley and beyond for miles. North White Plains Co-Town

Historian Sharon Tomback told *The Examiner News* in 2022 that "it's not entirely clear how the slope got its name, although it has been discussed among local historians that it may refer to the massacre of local Native Americans by the New Rochelle Huguenots at the site well before the Revolutionary War era." Historians are still searching for records of the possible Siwanoy massacre, which may have occurred before the reign of Sachem Wampage during the chieftaincy of Shonarocke.

 By October 23, 1776, trenches extended from the base of Mount Misery to the end of Orchard Street near the watershed and to the ridge of Hall Avenue, which turns into Buckout Road. The trenches were on raised terrain, protected on the right by the swampy ground near the Bronx River, with the two steep hills further back as a place of retreat. The American defenses were 3 miles long. Beyond that, on the right, was Chatterton Hill, which commanded the plain over which the British would have to advance. Several hundred militia men initially occupied the hill.

 On October 28, 1776, Howe's combined force of an estimated 13,000 British soldiers and Hessian mercenaries marched from Scarsdale towards White Plains. That afternoon, they clashed with Washington's estimated 14,500-strong army in what became known as The Battle of White Plains.

 Hundreds were killed or badly wounded in the bloody battle that pushed American troops off Battle Hill in downtown White Plains and Purdy Hill, now known as Church Street. Despite other local skirmishes beyond the central battle, General Howe's troops failed to gain ground on North Broadway or Lake Street.

On October 30, 1776, Washington's troops took positions on Mount Misery and Miller Hill, where part of the Continental Army encamped. Washington is said to have departed the Elijah Miller House during a rain storm the following night and relocated to Wright's Mills near the modern-day Kensico Dam.

On November 2, the British troops could not advance on Lake Street. They then proceeded along North Broadway to Cemetery Road and eventually took positions on Travis Hill, adjacent to the modern-day North White Plains train station. However, the fire from American cannons on higher Miller Hill forced the British soldiers off Travis Hill. As a result, the British ended their campaign on November 4 and returned to New York City.

In 1778, two years after his first visit, George Washington returned to the Elijah Miller House and stayed there for several weeks. He visited again in 1781. Some historians believe he entertained Marquis de Lafayette and General Rochambeau during these visits. Perhaps they sat under the old sycamore tree on the house's front lawn, which still stands today and is over 300 years old.

During the early 1900s, the Miller House was privately owned and operated as a chicken farm by Charles Kaiser, who later became Armonk's postmaster and a feature writer for the early *North Castle News*.

Westchester County purchased the farmhouse in July 1917, renovated it, and opened it to the public a year later as a museum. The Miller House has numerous artifacts on display, including a mahogany table and two fiddle-back chairs purported to have been used by Washington. However, in 1975, a discovery prompted much controversy.

In September 1937, *The Daily Times* wrote that the New York Historical Society had unearthed an old hand-drawn map of White Plains. The map, drawn by Washington's cartographer Robert Erskine, marked the Jacoby Purdy House in White Plains as "Head Quarters" and the Elijah Miller House as "Gates" for Continental Army General Horatio Gates. This discovery led local historians to dig deeper, as, before this, nobody at the Westchester Historical Society had heard of Washington ever staying at the Jacob Purdy House.

The claim was especially odd as Jacob Purdy, who lived to an advanced age as one of White Plains' oldest residents and was a great admirer of Washington, never said so himself. The 1937 article explains that the word "Headquarters" on Robert Erskine's 1778 map may refer to something else:

At the start of the American Revolution, an organization of patriotic Minute Men, known as Townsend's Rangers, began to hold meetings at the Purdy House. At once, the house was called "the Headquarters House," the headquarters for the Minute Men. This title was too long; only a few months elapsed before, evidently, just the word "Headquarters" was used to indicate the structure that Robert Erskine so indicated on his map to distinguish the building from other landmarks. It is the writer's belief that the Purdy House was called

"Headquarters" before the house was ever even seen by George Washington.

While that explanation may be accurate, the controversy between which of the two houses General Washington used as his headquarters in 1776 continued for decades.

The Purdy House was purchased by Samuel Purdy, the father of Jacob Purdy, back in 1730. The house claimed to have been used by General Washington as his headquarters was originally on Spring Street, but by the 1950s, it had fallen into disrepair and became a hangout spot for vagrants. In the 1960s, the historical society intervened. The house was renovated and restored, and in 1973, it was moved to its current location on 60 Park Avenue in White Plains, between Ferris Avenue and Church Street.

While the Battle of White Plains headquarters controversy continued, shortly after the restoration of the Purdy House, the Westchester Historical Society disclosed papers it received through the Library of Congress to prove that Washington stayed at the house for two months in 1778. The papers ironically originated with British female spy Anne Bates, who reported to Sir Henry Clinton in 1778, "General Washington's quarters at Mrs. Purdy's house to the left of the lines."

In 1975, the Elijah Miller House on Virginia Road reopened after a brief closure for remodeling. *The Reporter Dispatch* wrote about the reopening, which led to a subsequent article that addressed a purported error: the Jacob Purdy House was Washington's headquarters, not the Miller House.

The article stated that both houses were historically significant and that local historical organizations should collaborate to disseminate local history accurately. Despite the author being authoritative Westchester Historical Society leader Renoda Hoffman, the controversy between the two houses continued and remains unsolved.

The Elijah Miller House became listed on the National Register of Historic Places in 1976. Despite this, by the early 21st century, the historic site had deteriorated from decades of neglect and was minimally open to the public.

In 2010, the county legislature passed a $1.2 million bond issue to finance its restoration. However, the County Executive, who had previously supported preserving the historic site, vetoed the measure, saying private funds should support it. Due to the hard work of Friends of the Miller House & Washington's Headquarters and Daughters of Liberty's Legacy, Westchester County announced in May 2017 that up to $2 million of funds would be made available to renovate the house.

In 1979, the Jacob Purdy House became listed on the National Register of Historic Places. It's currently the headquarters of the Westchester Historical Society. Over the years, neighborhood residents have discovered numerous Revolutionary War artifacts at various local sites, including cannonballs and a bayonet recovered on Mount Misery.

18.) THE MYSTERIOUS OUTLAW

Despite General Washington residing in the neighborhood numerous times, perhaps at multiple locations, throughout the Revolutionary War, the local area mainly was deemed "The Neutral Ground" as it lay between the British Army based in Manhattan and the Continental Army based further north. As a result, the area became victimized by various marauding posses, including the most notorious, Delancey's Cowboys.

 As discussed at length in *Nightmarish Neighborhood #1*, Delancey's Cowboys, who also utilized the name The Westchester Chasseurs, were a gang of skilled fighters who rode on horseback throughout Westchester during the war, stealing from local Patriots and supporting the British Army. Many members were from Westchester, including their leader, James DeLancey, who turned on the American cause after several Patriots in White Plains stole his horse.

Many members joined DeLancey to disrupt the rebellion because of personal grudges. Captain Benjamin Ogden from North Castle had 200 acres of his land taken by the Patriots. Similarly, Colonel Isaac Hatfield, who refused to turn against the British Crown, was fined, imprisoned, and subsequently robbed by the Patriots, whom he declined to support.

While this rough group struck fear into local citizens, perhaps in a similar manner as infamous Wild West outlaws like Black Bart, Jesse James, Billy the Kid, and the Dalton Gang did a century later, Delancey's Cowboys did not believe they were doing anything wrong. They felt justified in looting cattle and goods from Patriot farms and providing those goods and supplies to the British Army. In their minds, perhaps their actions felt noble, like the actions of the folklore hero Robin Hood. However, some actions possibly were less noble as they were barbaric.

Sometimes, instead of stealing dry goods like flour, the Cowboys swiped people right out of their homes. On July 11, 1776, Judge John Thomas stood on the White Plains courthouse steps and read the Declaration of Independence to the public for the first time in New York State. Less than a year later, in March 1777, The Cowboys raided Judge Thomas' home in "Rye Woods" (West Harrison/Purchase border) and took him prisoner. They turned him over to British troops, who imprisoned him at the old Sugar House in New York City, where, on May 2, 1777, he died.

The judge's two sons joined the Patriot cause and became actively involved. Colonel Thomas Thomas commanded a Westchester regiment that frequently battled marauding groups like Delancey's Cowboys. John Thomas Jr. served in his brother's regiment and was High Sheriff of Westchester County.

Another dreaded crew that lurked in the neighborhood was The Queen's Rangers, led by the calculated John Graves Simcoe. In September 1778, they fought alongside Delancey's Cowboys, attacking rebels and taking prisoners.

In late October 1778, Simcoe's Rangers captured several cavalry regiments on King Street near the modern-day Westchester County Airport. The Rangers then took to looting and burning local stores.

In November 1778, Simcoe's Rangers raided Colonel Thomas' home near Rye Pond. As they approached the house, a shot was fired from inside, fatally striking a man by Simcoe's side. Another few inches and the man who would go on to become a national hero in Canada may have been shot dead near Old Orchard Street in North White Plains.

The man who fired the shot, James Brundage, was cruelly killed by The Queens Rangers shortly after they stormed the house. Like Judge Thomas, his son, Colonel Thomas, was also captured and turned over to British troops. They locked him away in a New York City prison and eventually freed him in a prisoner exchange.

The Cowboys perhaps targeted Colonel Thomas because New York Governor George Clinton had previously directed him to assist in removing livestock and grain from Westchester County to prevent it from falling into the enemy's hands. Part of the massive Thomas estate eventually became the campus of SUNY Purchase.

Early in 1780, nearly 300 Continental Army troops were stationed on King Street at the home of a Quaker named John Crummell, near the Quaker Meeting House in Harrison. Some of these troops clashed with DeLancey's Cowboys, ending in a bloody bayonet battle that wounded many.

During the war, a young North White Plains couple, the Fishers, were both heart and soul enlisted in the patriotic cause. Mr. Fisher was an efficient and active local militia member under John Paulding, one of the men who apprehended British spy Major Andre. His active duties as a scout sometimes kept him away from his farm for months, where his young wife had nothing but her heroism of spirit to oppose the roving bands of land pirates that stalked the Neutral Ground.

Mr. Fisher and his militia had a frightening encounter with a group of almost 300 Hessian mercenaries near Cooney Hill, which is near the Westchester County Airport, near Great Island. The locals feared the highly-trained, terrorizing German soldiers who fought alongside the British Army.

However, the local militia knew the rocky terrain well and used it to their advantage to launch a stealthy attack against the much larger enemy. They were stationed at different points and protected by jagged rocks. The smaller militia managed to scare the Hessians, forcing them to retreat from the area in panic.

During the Battle of White Plains, when the army of General Washington was camped near the Fisher's house, Mrs. Fisher fearlessly offered aid to the wounded and dying. She was always prepared to defend herself and assist others during emergencies. General Washington himself expressed gratitude to her.

On one occasion, DeLancey's Cowboys stole her favorite horse. Mrs. Fisher responded by riding to their camp in Morrisania and demanding it returned. Other times, she successfully hid local Patriots as they fled from Tory bandits. The marauders had a reputation for torturing victims until they surrendered property, including gold. One method was to tie a man into a chair and light a fire underneath him until he submitted to their demands. Once, she hid her husband under the house's floorboards to avoid detection.

Despite the multiple savage acts from Delancey's Cowboys, Simcoe's Rangers, and others, there was easily one individual with the reputation of the absolute baddest man in town: Shubael Merritt.

Patriarch Thomas Merritt defended the British Crown. After fighting in the Battle of Lexington, the Patriots captured Thomas Merritt Sr. on April 19, 1775. However, he managed to escape. Perhaps his political views and war stories influenced the decisions of two of his sons, Shubael and his older brother Thomas Jr.

Born in 1759, Thomas Jr. wanted to be a physician and studied at Harvard. Upon settling with his family in Rye, NY, he joined a newly formed unit under German officer Captain Andreas Emerich.

In May 1778, armed with rifles and dressed in green coats, Emerich's Chasseurs became a prominent faction defending the British Crown throughout The Neutral Ground. Perhaps their most infamous campaign was their involvement in the ambush and slaying of a Patriot militia comprised of Wappingers.

After the unit dissolved due to internal drama, Thomas Merritt Jr. became a member of Simcoe's Rangers, whose leader was impressed with the young officer.

On February 26, 1781, Merritt was with a Sergeant and 10 Rangers while providing cover for a foraging party. They fell in with a much larger group of militia from whom, after a series of charges back and forth, they managed to escape with the loss of the Sergeant killed. Merritt was knocked from his horse and left for dead. When he recovered, the field was empty. He made his way back to Georgetown without his boots, helmet, and weapons, which the militia had taken.

A month later, Thomas and about 20 others were captured and held in a small, dark place made of logs called a bullpen. He immediately organized his fellow prisoners, led them in a successful escape, and brought the party 50 miles to British-controlled territory. To Simcoe's relief, Thomas declined to offer a lieutenant position in another corps as a reward.

Thomas was a saint compared to his younger brother. Nowadays, most 17-year-old guys are focused on their senior year of high school, hanging out with friends, and maybe thinking about the prom. At age 17, Shubael joined Emmerich's Chasseurs. Their 1778 muster roll lists his occupation as a farmer and has him living on King Street in Rye.

After the unit disbanded, he joined Delancey's Cowboys. Through various heinous and violent acts, whether alone or with comrades, the teenager quickly grew a reputation as Westchester's most feared outlaw.

Shubael's nephew, Abe Merritt, talked with *Harper's Monthly Magazine* in 1879 and, when asked about his uncle, said, "He just sort of robbed and killed onto his account." He then told a story about his grandfather, who had a pair of shoe buckles that Shubael wanted.

"Shubael he say to my grandfather - as was called Bungy Joe on account of having invented a bunghole - he say that he want them shoe buckles, and so he tied the ole man's legs together and let him down into a well so as he could remember where they were. Then he'd draw him up, Shubael would ask him if he could remember better, so as the ole man was nigh about drowend afore he could make up his mind to tell Shubael where the things was."

On another occasion, Shubael allegedly robbed his younger brother Neamiah, who fled to Nova Scotia shortly after. During a raid, Shubael came near burning John Crummell to death for not telling him where he hid his money. Both George Washington and Lafayette had previously been guests in Crummell's home.

Another time, Shubael followed two French guys he saw on King Street. Alarmed by his suspicious appearance, the men fled across a field, prompting Shubael to fire at one of them. Shubael robbed the dead man, seizing a large sum of gold. The other man escaped and hid in a family's cellar on King Street. Despite Shubael not apprehending his target, he did enter the house and invite himself to the family's dinner.

Unfortunately, according to local legend, Shubael's antics grew more gruesome. After playing cards with his buddy Quail from Connecticut at a local watering hole, Shubael spotted local farmer Jonathan Kniffin plowing his field as his young son looked on. Shubael took his gun and shot Mr. Kniffin through the heart, instantly killing him in front of his son.

Abe Merritt told *Harpers* that the Merritt family settled in Virginia after being driven out of France before settling in New York in 1673. He references his great-grandfather William Merritt, the third Mayor of New York, and says that after his political career, he bought a house in Harrison's Purchase, where he later died. He also mentions that his grandmother, a member of the extensive Westchester Brundage family, many of whom resided in North Castle and in the lost village of Kensico, gave Major Andre directions to Tarrytown after his secret meeting with Benedict Arnold.

Despite Thomas and Shubael Merritt's variety of affairs during the war, whether legitimate or exaggerated over time, one perhaps stands out the most. According to long-forgotten local legend, the Merritt brothers almost captured General George Washington.

Thomas Merritt's grandson backed this story, stating,
"My grandfather has told me that once, at the head of an adequate force, he was within half an hour of capturing General George Washington himself and that a certain deacon, whose name I cannot now remember, was the cause of their failure, by giving the General information."

Perhaps the incident Thomas Merritt's grandson speaks of is connected to or led to one written about by Washington himself. On May 17,

1781, Washington wrote to Congress:

"Surprised near Croton River by 60 Horse and 200 foot under James DeLancey- 44 killed, wounded, and missing - attempted to cut him off, but he got away."

Another possibility is a January 1780 incident in which numerous groups, including Simcoe's Rangers, launched simultaneous attacks on Continental Army outposts and headquarters in New Jersey to abduct Washington. However, spies and stormy winter weather foiled the plans.

What became of the Merritt brothers remains a mystery. According to family tradition, in 1782, Thomas and his wife relocated to New Brunswick before returning to Westchester in 1790 and eventually settling near present-day St. Catharines, Canada, upon the recommendation of John Graves Simcoe. In 1803, Thomas became sheriff of the Niagara District and executive of the local agricultural society.

Shubael's fate is much more mysterious. There are multiple stories about his death. One local version is that the son of farmer Kniffin, who witnessed Shubael killing his father, avenged his dad's death by fatally shooting the outlaw.

Another version is that one of Shubael's robbery victims, named Holcomb, perhaps the French man who hid from Shubael in a cellar, mortally wounded Shubael during a shootout at a New Rochelle tavern. The Merritt family bible, however, states that Shubael and his wife, Letitia, returned to the family property after the war. In 1783, a party of

Whigs surprised Shubael at his house, dragged him outside, and shot him to death.

While Shubael Merritt's fate remains unknown, an authoritative clue comes from correspondence sent to George Washington in March 1779. The papers describe Shubael's court proceedings after his arrest.

The papers mention his involvement in cockfighting, horse stealing, and his role with Delancey's Cowboys in the raid on the Thomas house. However, the main charge against Shubael is perhaps a bit shocking: espionage.

Witnesses frequently saw Shubael coming within American lines in New York and Connecticut and "in a secret manner returning again to the enemies of the United States," so the court charged Shubael with being a spy.

The end of the report states: "After much deliberation, do unanimously judge the prisoner, Shubael Merritt, to be guilty of the charge exhibited against him and do adjudge him to suffer death by being hung by the neck until he shall be dead."

A large white oak tree, known as the treaty oak, stood on North Broadway by the intersection of Virginia Road, in front of a Revolutionary tavern called The Old Oak Inn, next to the Fisher family farm in North White Plains. Legend says that the historic tree was used by Continental soldiers to hang deserters and spies during the Revolution, earning it the nickname "The Old Washington Oak."

In September 1912, the old oak tree, which may have been where Westchester's once baddest outlaw met his fate, was destroyed in a storm. The tree, which for years marked the boundary of White Plains and North White Plains, was estimated to be over 500 years old.

The outside of the Oak Tree Inn has been the site of several fatalities, including the death of local resident John McNamee, whose body was found in the road outside the Inn in June 1907 by a milkman named Cuatt. Mr. McNamee worked for John Raven of Kensico at the family's hotel on Old Orchard Street for about 20 years.

In September 1917, Oak Tree Inn owner Otto May's five-year-old daughter Helen May was fatally struck by an automobile as she crossed North Broadway in front of the tavern. A few years later, White Plains couple Mr. and Mrs. Stephen Vivian died in a tragic automobile accident at the corner of Virginia Road and North Broadway.

The famous Oak Tree Inn survived until January 1921, when a fire of unknown origin destroyed it, just two weeks after state troopers discovered a quantity of illegitimate booze in the Inn's cellar during a raid. The tavern site is now Saveway Drycleaners, next door to the North White Plains firehouse.

Whether or not the Old Oak Tree was the execution site of Shubael Merritt remains unknown. Adding to the mystery of the infamous outlaw's life is a primarily illegible addendum to his court judgment, written by Continental Army Major Alexander McDougall, saying he has yet to approve Shubael's sentence, which leads us to a perhaps wild never-before-explored possibility.

What if Shubael Merritt wasn't an outlaw at all? What if he was a spy, not for the British, as charged, but instead an elite spy for General George Washington?

It's possible that playing a simple game of "What Do We Know?" could shed some light on the matter. We know that Shubael Merritt joined Emmerich's Chasseurs at the age of 17, and we also know that internal conflict ultimately led to the unit's destruction. The Americans, including Shubael, and the Germans, such as Emmerich, frequently disagreed, which resulted in the group - whose primary objective was to wreak havoc on the Patriots - being disbanded. Given this information, is it unrealistic to believe that if Shubael was, in fact, one of Washington's spies, he might have purposely contributed to the downfall of this enemy group from within?

We know that Shubael had a reputation for being an outlaw; however, what we know is based on stories instead of hard facts. A source of this information, including Shubael shooting farmer Kniffin and the French man with the gold, comes from Spencer Mead's 1911 book *Ye Historie of Yet Town of Greenwich*. What's interesting is after the publication of this book, Thomas Merritt's grandson, the same man who said the Merritt brothers were within a half hour of capturing George Washington, not only wrote that Shubael never killed anyone but also wrote that he brought this to Spencer Mead's attention numerous times and that Mr. Mead had agreed to correct the issue.

What's also a bit eye-catching is that Mr. Mead's book, which discusses Shubael shooting Farmer Kniffin, also discusses Farmer Kniffin's unnamed daughter.

"Some days ago, the daughter of Mr. Jonathan Kniff of Rye in Connecticut was murdered by a Party of Rebels near or upon Budd's Neck. She was carrying some clothes to her father, in the company of two men who had the charge of a herd of cattle. They were fired upon by the Rebels from behind a stone wall. The poor young woman received a ball in her head, of which she instantly died. The men escaped unhurt. They plundered her dead body off its clothes, cut one of her fingers almost off to take a ring, and left the corpse most indecently exposed on the highway. Such are the advocates of this cursed Rebellion!"

It's unclear what the Kniffin family's role in the Revolution was, if any. However, it's perhaps strange that Shubael, portrayed as an outlaw and Loyalist, attacked Mr. Kniffin while a group of Patriots fatally shot his unarmed daughter and violated her corpse.

We know that Merritt family tradition says the Merritt boys were within a half hour of capturing Washington. We also know that Simcoe's Rangers tried to capture Washington in 1780, and DeLancey's Cowboys tried in 1781. We also know that both attempts didn't go according to plan, and according to Thomas Merritt's grandson, some mystery person alerted a deacon, who tipped off Washington of the plan. Could that mystery person have been a spy working undercover?

We know that Abe Merritt described Shubael as an outlaw who would rob and kill; however, if Shubael was really a spy who perhaps stealthily relocated to somewhere like Canada after the Revolution, is it possible his descendants in the know just kept up the ruse?

From the court papers, we know that witnesses frequently saw Shubael Merritt crossing from enemy lines into American lines in New York and Connecticut and then back. For this, he was arrested and charged as a spy for the British Crown and sentenced to death by hanging. Perhaps it was the work of an outlaw hunting prey, or maybe it was one of Washington's men working undercover. It remains unknown why Maj. Gen. Alexander McDougall stepped in with an addendum to the judgment, and there appears to be no record as to whether or not Shubael was executed by hanging or perhaps secretly released.

George Washington, the first president of the United States, also served as America's first intelligence chief during the Revolutionary War. He spent more than 10% of the military funding on intelligence activities, which included managing individual spies, running spy rings, and establishing special units for collecting military intelligence.

During the early years of the war, Washington personally supervised the recruitment, training, and management of intelligence agents. The most sophisticated of Washington's agent networks was the Culper Ring, established in the summer of 1778 in New York and consisting of about 20 people. They passed on information using aliases, coded writing, dead drops, and other tradecrafts.

Confirmed members included Benjamin Tallmadge, Robert Townshend, Sarah "Sally" Townshend, Caleb Brewster, and Anna Strong. Others, like 21-year-old Nathan Hale and Joshua Davis, were caught as spies and hanged by the British in 1776 before the Culper Spy Ring's formation.

Washington also utilized spies posing as things they weren't. For instance, James Armistead Lafayette was an African-American who posed as a runaway slave who agreed to work with the British, though, in actuality, he was collecting intelligence from the British and reporting it back to Patriot forces.

Washington emphasized the importance of human intelligence and provided intelligence tradecraft training to his field commanders. For example, on March 28, 1779, Washington wrote to Major General Alexander McDougall. In the letter, Washington warned McDougall's secret agent not to trust double spies and to be cautious until the agent had given full proof of their loyalty.

The British also had confirmed undercover spies, like Ann Bates. The Philadelphia school teacher and beekeeper was also the wife of a British soldier. She pretended to be a Patriot to gather and identify important information to send back to British forces. She walked into George Washington's White Plains headquarters and explained that she had observed and noted each brigade's strength, situation, and number of cannons. Bates' information influenced General Henry Clinton's decision to send more forces to defend Rhode Island, which led to American and French armies withdrawing from Newport.

While we don't know for certain, we know that Shuabel Merritt was perhaps a notorious outlaw, a British spy as charged, a double agent working for Washington, or maybe something else altogether. His life seems to be quite puzzling, especially the variety of conflicting stories regarding his death.

Local lore is that Shubael died in his early 20s, perhaps during a shootout or perhaps by a noose outside 615 North Broadway in North White Plains. It's believed that his family buried him in an orchard, believed to be at the edge of Doc Holladay's 100-acre estate, bordering Buckout Road, adjacent to Old Orchard Street. It remains unknown if Shubael Merritt was a bloodthirsty outlaw or perhaps one of history's most interesting young men whose story has yet to be fully told.

19.) JIMMY-UNDER-THE ROCK-

Throughout history, the North Castle area has been home to multiple men and women who lived in strange and isolated dwellings on the outskirts of town. Some of these individuals defied social norms to live as hermits and have become iconic figures, achieving legendary folklore-like status.

A local legend that has yet to be confirmed claims that religious reformer Anne Hutchinson resided briefly in a cave near Bear Gutter Creek, located just southwest of Armonk, during the 1640s. In later years, that cave was nicknamed "Heliker Cave" in honor of a Revolutionary War-era hermit named Bet Heliker. Excavations of Heliker's Cave, located in the woods near a now-closed bowling alley, revealed the discovery of Native American utensils and arrowheads.

Perhaps tales like these or that of Rye Lake's "Aunt" Betty Thompson, inspired a choice made by a local man named James Johnson, who, after engaging in a heated argument with his family, decided to leave home and relocate to the woods near the base of Mount Misery, in the woods past the intersection of modern Nethermont Avenue and Hillandale Street.

James created a unique rock shelter using an overgrown ravine with a large flat rock jutting about 20 feet, serving as his new roof. He constructed floors of local fieldstones and added rough, unfinished wood walls, complete with windows and a door. He put in a good-sized stove for cooking and heating.

To combat being attacked by local copperhead snakes, James bolted a bed made from the body of a box wagon to the cave ceiling. To climb into his elevated snake-proof bed, he used a 10-foot ladder, which he'd later withdraw upon tucking himself in.

As years passed, locals began referring to James by the nicknames "Hermit of the Rock" and the more popular "Jimmy Under The Rock." The eccentric individual chose to live solitary, except for his few animal friends, for whom he built rock barns. Jimmy kept goats, pigs, cows, chickens, and horses at his makeshift estate. The home's rock roof became a favorite climbing spot for the goats.

Although gruff in appearance and allegedly unfriendly to unwanted visitors, Jimmy was considered harmless. That, of course, didn't stop folks in the area from creating urban legends about him as the local boogeyman.

In the July 1939 issue of the *Quarterly Bulletin of the Westchester County Historical Society*, George Stevens said, "I am minded of the time over 60 years ago when, as a barefoot boy of 10 years, I used to pass by Jimmy's shelter. I was so fearful he would come out and catch me that my hair stood on end, and I ran so fast I surely made a speed record for a boy of that age."

In addition to raising animals, Jimmy enjoyed gardening. He lived off the land and a flourishing garden. His old white horse was used for plowing, carting, or transportation when Jimmy needed to go into White Plains for supplies. According to local legend, Jimmy rode out of town backward on his horse to wave goodbye to his city friends.

Being practically self-sufficient, Jimmy lived in this manner for many years, though only with some problems. The heavy rains often poured through his abode, leaving a steady stream across his floors. Even worse, the cold New York winter winds would easily creep through the numerous cracks and crevices of the building. Several times, he was found in his bed, nearly frozen to death. All efforts to entice him from his solitary life failed until, one day, things changed.

After surviving in his homemade rock shelter for many years, Jimmy finally evacuated his infamous rock home in 1877. A local North White Plains business owner, George Mead, owner of a popular bakery on Railroad Avenue, offered Jimmy a comfortable place to stay.

Jimmy resided with George Mead for about a year. One morning, shortly after finishing breakfast, Jimmy became suddenly ill and dropped dead. Coroner Frank Schirmer investigated, and the jury rendered a verdict of death by heart disease. Schirmer estimated that Jimmy was about 70 years old, though later articles about the iconic hermit place him at 90. Town records regarding Jimmy's death and burial site remain unfound.

Today, all that remains of Jimmy's legendary home is a large flat stone and a small portion of the foundation wall, about 2,000 feet directly east of the eastern end of Hillandale Avenue on the City of White Plains watershed property in North White Plains, in the direction of Rocky Ledge on Old Orchard Street.

Jimmy's legendary local lifestyle may have inspired a few others, including "James Street Jerry."

During the 1970s, neighbors in the Quarry Heights section of North White Plains fought for the eviction of a man named Jerry, who lived on James Street, off Old Orchard Street. Jerry lived in what his neighbors described as a dilapidated, unsanitary structure without running water, electricity, sewer facilities, or a certificate of occupancy. Eventually, the town of North Castle fought for six months to evict Jerry, stating his makeshift shack on a 60x80 foot lot constructed after a fire destroyed his house was "an unsafe eyesore." However, they lost their case despite their efforts.

The estate of "James Street Jerry" was located near the former residence of highly respected local blacksmith Harry McClure. During the early 1900s, Mr. McClure worked as a lion-tamer for the Barnum and Bailey Circus and later shooed horses for William Muldoon. In honor of the long-time resident, a street near Mr. McClure's James Street home was named McClure Place. After Harry's passing, members of his family resided in his two-story frame house until a fire destroyed it.

During the early 1970s, the Westchester County Department of Health received multiple complaints about more than two dozen junked cars nestled among the trees in approximately 16 acres of wooded town-owned property off Old Orchard Street. The highlight of the complaints was a shanty built with an overturned car as one of its walls.

20.) WESTMINSTER RIDGE

Across the street from George Washington Elementary School on Orchard Street is the intersection of Orchard and Garrettson Road. Less than half a mile up Garrettson Road is a small recreational area called Westminster Park. A.C. Todd built the park in 1912 and named its small pond after himself, Todd's Pond. Unfortunately, the pleasant recreational area became the site of tragedies.

In 1926, Fred Stafford and his wife bought one of the only four houses near Westminster Park. Three years later, the couple who initially lived in Briarcliff Manor purchased an additional 15 acres of surrounding property, including the pond.

Todd's Pond was a dumping ground for various debris at the time. Tree stumps, broken glass, and even busted parts from old automobiles littered its waters. After the Staffords led a project to clean out the pond, it became a place where children from a wide surrounding area would come to cool off, swim, and even dive.

In the succeeding months of development, the Staffords connected sewers, gas, and lights and completed the road adjacent to the pond, now called Garretson Road. The couple even paid the bill for street lighting in the area for several years before the city assumed the responsibility.

Unfortunately, in August 1927, 7-year-old Philip Bellantoni drowned in Todd's Pond. The local youth lived nearby on Kensico Avenue. His family had previously suffered multiple tragedies, including the drowning deaths of his grandparents, cousin, and aunt following an automobile accident two years prior on Thanksgiving Day, and the boy's uncle, who in 1917 was murdered.

In June 1928, 21-year-old Anthony Fraello, who lived on Ferris Avenue in White Plains, went swimming at Todd's Pond with five friends. Stricken with cramps, the young man drowned in six feet of water. City firefighters recovered his body six hours after the fatality.

Fred Stafford died in 1933. A few years later, an architect named Lee Perry purchased the Stafford's property and decided to transform the area around Todd's Pond into a colonial community, which he named Westminster Ridge.

Perry described the project in 1938 as a "low-cost, small home colony." He reasoned that if an architect can conceive one home, he should be able to plan an entire community. Excavation for the initial five development units began in February 1938, and they were sold before their completion in May. Afterward, Perry received orders for multiple more units in his Westminster Ridge development.

Perry explained, "I really got the low-cost bug in a big way last fall when I began to realize there was a distinct lack of proper housing in Westchester for the wage earner." As a result, Westminster Ridge houses vary in size and design. The tract is divided into 75 lots, five to an acre. Plots range from 50 by 100 feet to 100 by 150 feet. In 1938, many of the cottage-style houses, featuring four rooms, garage, bath, full cellar, and attic, sold for $6,000 (approx $132,000 in 2024). The slightly larger model, "The Lincoln," has six rooms, a bath, a garage, a cellar, a fireplace, and asbestos-made shingles and is sold in the $8,500 range.

 The neighborhood's proximity to the school, the community pond, and the recreational playground made it appealing to new homeowners. Perry's 15 acres quickly began to fill in. Less than three years after the first residents of Westminster Ridge moved into their new homes, residents of the new development threatened police action to curb consistent midnight swimming parties at Todd's Pond. At one party in July 1941, a rowboat ended up on top of the clubhouse on the pond's manufactured sandy shoreline.

 Todd's Pond eventually adopted the nickname "Laken Ridge Club" (Lake-en-ridge) by development residents who began showing off neighborhood pride. By the 1950s, Todd's Pond, now referred to as a lake, had local lifeguards on duty, like 17-year-old Elliot Enyedy of Garretson Road, who in 1957 rescued a drowning 9-year-old girl from the Laken Ridge Club's waters.

 Two weeks after New Year's 1964, a shocking, violent incident rocked the quiet Lakenridge community. Marital violence and death shattered the mid-day quiet of a Westminster Ridge dead-end street.

 27-year-old nurse Mrs. Linda Olmestead Paynter and her five-year-old son returned to her childhood home in Westminster Ridge after

separating from her husband, unemployed truck driver Richard Paynter.
Richard had numerous run-ins with the law, most recently a larceny
charge for stealing a car, which temporarily landed the Air Force
veteran in jail.

Shortly after release, 29-year-old Richard, who had been living with
his parents in Hawthorne, forced his way into the Olmstead's home.
Linda's New York attorney father was not home, and Richard's
reconciliation attempts with his wife quickly failed.

While arguing, Richard ripped the phone from the wall and chased
Linda with a kitchen carving knife. She screamed for her dad's helper,
later identified by police as "Chinese Perkins," to call for help from a
neighbor's phone. When the opportunity arose, Linda bolted from the
house and began sprinting down the road.

When the police arrived, they found Richard 100 feet from the house
on a snow bank, sobbing, calling his wife's name as he held a bent knife
over his wife's dead body. He told police he had tried to kill himself,
but the knife bent. The police arrested him for second-degree murder.

That summer, tragedy struck again. Despite lifeguards on duty and the
lake formerly known as Todd's Pond being closed after certain times,
late-night trespassing still occurred. In late June 1964, a group of 15
Westchester boys went swimming at the lake after dark. Around 10 pm,
17-year-old Theodore DeRuvo drowned while swimming. A man from
Garretson Road later found his body.

In February 1967, a firecracker tossed by a local youth ignited natural gas seeping from a main under the roadway, resulting in what folks in the area called "a burning wall." Residents reported the odor of leaking gas, and Consolidated Edison turned off the electricity in all homes bordering Garretson Road and Lake View Drive.

Perhaps ironically, fire officials reported that the eerily burning gas acted as a safety valve, preventing gas from accumulating under the roadway, building pressure, and possibly causing a significant explosion.

A string of burglaries occurred in Westminster Ridge during four weeks in 1978. The police believed that the same criminals committed all seven home invasions. The crooks struck during daylight hours, breaking in through unlocked storm windows and making off with easily transportable items.

During the late 1990s, a Westminster Ridge sign made of Styrofoam designed to look like stone was placed across the street from George Washington School near a mailbox at the Orchard St and Garretson Road intersection. While investigating multiple reports of vehicle break-ins in the neighborhood, the police removed the sign.

Despite the lack of a sign and numerous tragedies, Westminster Ridge, which began as a low-cost housing project, has been a pleasant neighborhood for many who have lived there. It's perhaps a tad ironic, however, that such a pleasant-looking development of colonial homes surrounding a sandy-shored lake backs up into a street that has been the subject of urban legends, eerie history, and spooky hauntings, earning it the nickname of America's scariest street, Buckout Road.

Additional books from the *Nightmarish Neighborhood* series are available now on Amazon and BarnesAndNoble.com.

For more info, please visit: RightOnDudes.com